Economics

Economics

Volume 4

The U.S. economy and the world

GROLIER
EDUCATIONAL

Sherman Turnpike,
Danbury, Connecticut
06816

Published 2000 by Grolier Educational
Sherman Turnpike
Danbury, Connecticut 06816

© 2000 Brown Partworks Ltd

Set ISBN: 0-7172-9492-7
Volume ISBN: 0-7172-9485-4

Library of Congress Cataloging-in-Publication Data
Economics.
     p. cm.
     Includes index.
     Contents: v. 1 Money, banking, and finance — v. 2.
Business operations — v. 3. The citizen and the
economy — v. 4. The U.S. economy and the world —
v. 5. Economic theory — v. 6. History of economics
     ISBN 0-7172-9492-7 (set: alk. paper). — ISBN 0-7172-
9482-X (v. 1: alk. paper). — ISBN 0-7172-9483-8 (v. 2:
alk. paper). — ISBN 0-7172-9484-6 (v. 3: alk. paper). —
ISBN 0-7172-9485-4 (v. 4: alk. paper). — ISBN 0-7172-
9570-2 (v. 5: alk. paper). — ISBN 0-7172-9571-0 (v. 6:
alk. paper).
     1. Economics—Juvenile literature [1. Economics.] I.
Grolier Educational Corporation.

HB183. E26 2000
330—dc21   00-020414

For information address the publisher:
Grolier Educational, Sherman Turnpike,
Danbury, Connecticut 06816

FOR BROWN PARTWORKS LTD

Project editor:
Jane Lanigan
Editors: Tim Cooke, Julian
Flanders, Mike Janson,
Henry Russell
Editorial assistance:
Wendy Horobin,
Tim Mahoney,
Sally McEachern,
Chris Wiegand
Design: Tony Cohen,
Bradley Davis,
Matthew Greenfield
Picture research:
Helen Simm
Graphics: Mark Walker
Indexer:
Kay Ollerenshaw

Project consultant: Robert
Pennington, Associate
Professor, College of
Business Administration,
University of Central
Florida
Text: Richard Widdows,
Michael Oliver, Nick
Mathiason, Mike Janson

About this book

Economics is all around us. It covers almost
every aspect of life today, from how much
money you have in your pocket to the price of
real estate, from how much tax people pay to
the causes of wars in distant lands. In today's
world it is essential to understand how to manage your money, how to save wisely, and how
to shop around for good deals. It is also important to know the bigger picture: how financial
institutions work, how wealth is created and
distributed, how economics relates to politics,
and how the global economy works that ties
together everyone on the planet.

Economics places everyday financial
matters in the wider context of the sometimes
mysterious economic forces that shape our
lives, tracing the emergence of economic doc-
trines and explaining how economic systems
worked in the past and how they work now.

Each of the six books covers a particular area of economics, from personal finance to
the world economy. Five books are split into
chapters that explore their themes in depth.
Volume 5, Economic Theory, is arranged as an A-
Z encyclopedia of shorter articles about fundamental concepts in economics and can be used
as an accessible reference when reading the
rest of the set. At the end of every chapter or
article a See Also box refers you to related articles elsewhere in the set, allowing you to further investigate topics of particular interest.

The books contain many charts and
diagrams to explain important data clearly and
explain their significance. There are also special
boxes throughout the set that highlight particular subjects in greater detail. They might explain
how to fill out a check correctly, analyze the
theory proposed by a particular economist, or
tell a story that shows how economic theory
relates to events in our everyday lives.

If you are not sure where to find a
subject, look it up in the set index in each
volume. The index covers all six books, so it
will help you trace topics throughout the set.
There is also a glossary at the end of the book,
which provides a brief explanation of some of
the key words and phrases that occur throughout the volumes. The extensive Further Reading
list contains many of the most recent books
about different areas of economics to allow you
to do your own research. It also features a list
of useful web sites where you can find up-to-
date information and statistics.

Contents

The U.S. economy and the world

The U.S. government and world economics

The United States has the world's largest and most dominant economy. This is partly because its economic and political structures make efficient use of great natural resources, but mainly because of a long-term policy to establish itself as the world's banker and policeman.

Economic and political relations between the United States and the rest of the world have crucially affected the course of history ever since the nation achieved independence from Britain at the end of the 18th century. As a young nation the United States sought to free itself from the influence of European powers by a policy of developing trade with and amassing territory from those powers. For much of the 19th century the nation's internal westward expansion was accompanied by further attempts to exclude European powers from North and South American affairs. Little more than 100 years after its creation under principles of republicanism and international peace, economic and strategic considerations had made the United States a colonial power in the Caribbean and the Pacific. The early 20th century saw the United States attempt to remain aloof from international affairs, even though it was eventually drawn into the two world wars. Likewise, during the Great Depression of the 1930s the nation responded to international crisis by erecting a barrier of tariffs to protect its own national economy. This all changed after 1945.

The global role of the United States

Confirmed by World War II as the world's economic superpower and the defender of democracy and capitalism against communism and dictatorship, the United States was heavily involved in foreign affairs throughout the period of the Cold War. Its involvement in the conflict in Vietnam in particular had a profound effect on the U.S. economy and, eventually, on how Americans see themselves.

Today the United States has the world's strongest economy and has become its great international benefactor and policeman. Any country that conducts its internal affairs in a way that the United States wants or needs to support will benefit from substantial trade advantages such as those currently enjoyed by Israel and Croatia. By contrast, nations

The Monroe Doctrine, Latin America, and the OAS

ABOVE: The fifth President of the United Sates, James Monroe was born in Westmoreland County, Virginia, in 1758 and died in New York City in 1831.

By pledging U.S. assistance to any country on the American continent that was threatened by a European power, the Monroe Doctrine introduced the notion of collective security and cooperation throughout all the Americas. This idea became a constant of U.S. policy in the 19th and 20th centuries, and provided the justification for many U.S.-backed initiatives throughout the region. They included mutual defense treaties, regional economic aid programs, and pan-American conferences. This part of the Monroe Doctrine was eventually formalized and codified in the Organization of American States (OAS), which was founded in 1948.

governed by regimes of which the United States disapproves may be subjected to severe economic sanctions and even military intervention. Iraq, Libya, and the former Yugoslav republic of Serbia are among the countries against which the United States has taken decisive action of both types.

The Monroe Doctrine

The United States' present international economic dominance is the result of a long evolution from the nation born in a revolutionary war against an imperial power. The later stages of the war against Britain from 1775 to 1783 allied American patriots with France, Spain, and the Netherlands. Even before it came into being, therefore, the new nation could not ignore its role as part of a network of European colonies in North America. Its European allies fought largely for European causes, seeing the defeat of Britain as a chance for increasing their own territorial or trade empires in the New World.

By the 1783 Treaty of Paris Britain retained the northern territories of Canada; Spain governed Florida, Mexico—which extended north to Oregon and east to Louisiana—and Louisiana, which it ceded to France in 1800. In the west Russia controlled fur-rich Alaska.

Although the new nation saw itself as turning its back on international rivalries in favor of cooperation and peace, it was at once drawn into the affairs of the colonial powers. A similar contradiction between an intention to remain isolated and an imperative to become involved has often marked U.S. foreign relations. Despite great public sympathy for the republican aims of the French Revolution that started in 1789, secretary of the treasury Alexander Hamilton supported Great Britain in the Napoleonic Wars that followed in order to protect U.S. trade. By the Jay Treaty of 1794 Britain granted U.S. shipping the protection of its Royal Navy in return for U.S. acceptance of its naval supremacy. The treaty angered many patriots and nearly brought the United States to a naval war with France.

ABOVE: The Battle of Cerro Gordo, fought on April 18, 1847, was one of the key engagements of the U.S.-Mexican War of 1846 to 1848.

Porfirio Díaz

The economic and political influence of the United States in Mexico increased greatly after Porfirio Díaz became president of its southern neighbor in 1876 at the age of 46. Díaz's dictatorship helped the U.S. government and companies to establish complete commercial control of his country.

Like many of his fellow countrymen, this former priest, lawyer, and soldier regarded the United States as Mexico's archenemy following bitter wars between the two countries 30 years previously. He once complained that his country was "so far from God, so close to the United States." Díaz was determined to raise the living standards of his people, however, and for that he needed U.S. help. The president provided incentives for U.S. investment and political stability. By 1910 the United States had pumped more than $2 billion into Mexican mining, petroleum, railroads, and agriculture. U.S. firms controlled 850 of the 1,000 foreign mining firms that were operating in Mexico by 1908.

Díaz brutally appropriated lands belonging to peasant farmers, but thanks to him, Mexico now had a 19,000-mile-network of railroads and an efficient postal and telegraph service. Within Mexico, however, Díaz was criticized for being "the tool of the Yankee." His regime created a hatred of foreigners among his population because they saw U.S. companies taking profits out of Mexico rather than reinvesting them in the country.

Mexicans had other reasons for dissatisfaction under Díaz. First, they lost 900,000 square miles of their territory to encroaching U.S. businesses. Second, Díaz operated a dual wage system under which U.S. workers got twice as much money as Mexican workers for the same job. This inequality culminated in a strike at the Cananea Copper Mine in 1906. Rather than send in the Mexican army to restore order, Díaz did nothing. This allowed the U.S. mine-owner, Colonel Greene, to call in U.S. forces, who killed many Mexican workers.

Just over four years later Diaz was swept from power in a revolution. He died in exile in 1915, but his legacy of U.S. business involvement in Mexico would remain important much longer.

ABOVE: *Born in 1830, Porfirio Díaz served two terms as president of Mexico, from 1877 to 1880 and from 1884 to 1911. He died in Paris, France.*

The presidency of Thomas Jefferson from 1800 to 1809 was marked by a policy of U.S. expansion in North America. In 1803 Jefferson doubled the size of the United States when he bought the vast Louisiana Territory from the French emperor Napoleon, who could not afford to defend the region. He sent Meriwether Lewis and William Clark to explore a route across the Louisiana Purchase to the Pacific. Jefferson also set underway the negotiations that ended in 1819 with the purchase of Florida from Spain.

Jefferson's expansion needed an economic foundation in increased trade, but events in Europe made it difficult. With Britain and France engaged in the Napoleonic Wars, both tried to stifle the other side's trade with the United States, often by seizing U.S. ships and their cargoes. Jefferson embargoed trade with both nations from 1807 to 1809, with

catastrophic consequences for American commerce. Jefferson's successor, James Madison, declared war on Britain in 1812; British troops overran Washington, D.C., burning the White House and the Capitol. The war damaged U.S. trade so badly that New England separatists tried to withdraw the northern states from the conflict to protect their business interests. After a series of American naval victories the war ended with the 1814 Treaty of Ghent, bringing to an end a half-century of conflict with Britain.

Early in the 19th century countries in Latin America declared their independence from Spain, including in 1821 both Mexico and Colombia. The United States and other countries, including Britain, were concerned that the Spanish would try to restore their rule in the region, closing again the lucrative markets that had opened. Britain suggested that the

AROUND THE WORLD
THROUGH THE PANAMA CANAL
Two Grand Cruises by Sister Ships
"CINCINNATI," January 16, 1915
and
"CLEVELAND," January 31, 1915
From New York to the principal cities of the world — including a visit to the San Diego (Cincinnati) and Panama Pacific (Cleveland) Exposition
135 DAYS $900 UP including all necessary expenses afloat and ashore
HAMBURG - AMERICAN LINE
41-45 Broadway, New York
Philadelphia   Boston   Baltimore   Pittsburgh   Chicago

British and Americans issue a joint declaration against future colonization in Latin America. Secretary of state John Quincy Adams, worried that Britain might use its fleet to prevent a Spanish expedition and that the United States would be a "cock boat behind the British man-of-war," insisted that the Americans should issue their own declaration.

In 1823 President James Monroe outlined the principles that became known as the Monroe Doctrine, which shaped future U.S. relations with Europe and Latin America (*see* box, page 6). The three main principles of the doctrine were that there should be no further European colonization of the New World, that the United States should refrain from involvement in the political affairs of Europe, and that the United States would view as a hostile act any European intervention in the governments of the American hemisphere.

Keeping Europe at a safe distance

The Monroe Doctrine—which drew on ideas previously set out in George Washington's valedictory address and Thomas Jefferson's Inaugural—implied that U.S. strategic and economic interests went hand in hand with those of its neighbors. It marked the first formal expression of the United States' intention to dominate the affairs of a continent on which potentially hostile European interests were still represented in Canada by the British, the world's foremost naval and economic power, in Alaska by Russia, which had declared a ban on all non-Russian ships from the Northwest coast, in Cuba by the Spanish themselves, and in Brazil by the Portuguese.

ABOVE: The opening of the Panama Canal in 1914 enabled round-the-world liners to avoid Cape Horn on journeys from the Atlantic to the Pacific—a short cut that saved 8,000 miles.

RIGHT: Work in progress on the Gaillard (Culebra) Cut of the 51-mile Panama Canal. Today ships typically take between 15 and 20 hours to navigate the whole length of the canal.

LEFT: Theodore Roosevelt, the 26th President of the United States, was earlier one of the most enthusiastic supporters of the war with Spain in Cuba, where he commanded a band of U.S. volunteers, the famed Roughriders.

Monroe was trying to exclude European influence from the New World. In fact, the doctrine had little short-term practical effect. It was little more than an act of bravado by a young nation against European states that in any case, had no plans to intervene in the region. The United States made few moves to ally itself with its Latin American neighbors, which, partly as a result, became more economically dependent on Britain.

The Mexican War (1846–1848)

The expansionist tendencies inherent in the Monroe Doctrine were evident during the presidency of James K. Polk from 1844 to 1849. Polk claimed that "manifest destiny" made it the United States' divine right to control the whole continent. In 1846 he threatened hostilities with Britain to claim part of Oregon. From 1846 to 1848 he went to war with Mexico, originally over the boundaries of Texas, recently incorporated into the Union. With victory the United States acquired over 500,000 square miles of Mexican territory from the Rio Grande to the Pacific Ocean: the land subsequently became the states of California,

Nevada, Utah, most of Arizona, and parts of Wyoming, Colorado, and New Mexico. In the 1853 Gadsden Purchase the United States bought land from Mexico south of the Gila River, establishing the southern border of the modern United States. The United States would buy Alaska from Russia in 1867, by which time the lucrative fur seal was virtually extinct in the region.

From civil war to world power

The mid-19th century also saw U.S. moves to establish a trading presence in East Asia. In 1853 Commodore Matthew Perry led four U.S. warships into the harbor in Edo, Japan, to force the isolationist country to open its ports to foreign trade. Within four years Japan's jealously guarded isolation disappeared as it opened its ports and set low import taxes to allow foreign businesses to make high profits.

The American Civil War (1861–1865) gave foreign powers an opportunity to muscle in on the U.S. sphere of interest. France attempted to occupy Mexico and absorb it under the rule of Archduke Maximilian. When Mexican rebels overthrew Maximilian, U.S. Secretary of

State William Seward cited the Monroe Doctrine in a clear threat against interference, and French forces backed off.

After the Civil War the United States experienced rapid economic growth that made it one of the world's major powers. Although the Monroe Doctrine suggested that the United States would remain aloof from European affairs and international squabbles, many Americans now believed that the country should start acting like the international power it had become. In addition, many Americans feared that the disappearance of the land frontier with the settlement of the Pacific Coast meant that U.S. commerce needed to find new markets.

War with Spain

American attention turned to Cuba, one of the Caribbean possessions by which the Spanish retained their presence in the Americas. In 1895 Cuban rebels launched an unsuccessful revolution that was put down by the island's Spanish rulers. Whipped up by the popular press and the sinking of a U.S. ship in Havana harbor—later revealed to have been caused by an accident—the government of President William McKinley sent U.S. troops to expel the Spanish from Cuba. It took only months for the American troops to drive Spain from Cuba and its last Caribbean possession, Puerto Rico. As part of the peace settlement McKinley forced the Spanish to "sell" the United States their Pacific possessions in the Philippines. The United States had become an imperial power, although antiimperialists at once expressed their doubts about the enterprise, for example, making Cuba a U.S. protectorate rather than part of the United States itself.

The possession of the Philippines made the United States an important power in the Pacific. Britain, France, Russia, and Japan had in the 1890s divided up the potentially lucrative market of China. In 1898 and 1899 the United States proposed an Open Door policy to those powers, allowing equal trading rights to all. The United States also committed itself to protecting China's integrity and was thus involved in, for example, mediating the Russo-Japanese War in 1905.

The Roosevelt Corollary

The early 20th century saw the United States extending its direct influence over its neighbors. Its government was eager to build a canal across the Central American isthmus to provide a shorter route for goods and navy vessels between the Atlantic Coast and California. This it eventually did by sending gunboats to separate Panama from Colombian rule in 1903. Building the canal through disease-ridden swamps was a major engineering

ABOVE: Copper mines in the Andes Mountains of Chile. The United States has always been eager to safeguard its access to the enormous natural resources of Latin America.

feat: when it was opened in 1914, the Panamanian economy became totally reliant on that of the United States.

In 1904 Britain, Germany, Italy, and the Netherlands threatened to intervene in Venezuela and the Dominican Republic to collect debts owed to their own nationals. In response U.S. President Theodore Roosevelt set out what became known as the Roosevelt Corollary to the Monroe Doctrine. It articulated the right of the United States to act as an "international police power" wherever "chronic wrong-doing or an impotence which results in general loosening of the ties of civilized society" required intervention "by some civilized nation." From this developed the role of the United States as the world's policeman. Roosevelt himself described his approach as "big stick diplomacy," a quote from an African proverb to the effect that one should "speak softly and carry a big stick."

Throughout the 20th century the United States has been generally strongly interventionist in foreign affairs: the Roosevelt Corollary has led to numerous interventions and occupations in regions all over the world, from Nicaragua to Vietnam. U.S. policy rests on two foundations, one pragmatic, the other idealistic. The first is simple economic and strategic self-interest; the second is America's visions of itself as the standard-bearer for democracy and freedom, values perceived as being threatened particularly after 1945 by Soviet-inspired communism.

Revolution in Mexico

In 1911 Porfirio Díaz resigned from the presidency of Mexico, which he had ruled as a virtual dictator for 35 years (*see* box, page 8).

Díaz's presidency had brought great U.S. investment in Mexico. At the time of his resignation Americans owned three-quarters of Mexico's mines and rubber plantations and half of its oil. Mexico was in the midst of a revolution, however. Díaz's uncompromising rule made him unpopular with many Mexicans. Poor rural peasants, supported by the middle classes, fought to regain what had once been common land but under Díaz had passed into the hands of great landowners.

As a succession of Mexican presidents took power and lost it, U.S. President Woodrow Wilson had to judge how best to protect U.S. trade interests by achieving stability. In 1913 Victoriano Huerta seized power in a coup, murdering his predecessor. Revolts against him continued into the next year, led by the bandits Emiliano Zapata and Pancho Villa and by the politician Venustiano Carranza, whose call for a return to constitutional government was supported by Wilson. In 1914 Wilson used a fragile excuse to send U.S. troops to occupy the Mexican port of Veracruz, cutting off customs duties that were vital revenue for Huerta's government and irreparably weakening his position.

Huerta fled into exile in July 1914, and Carranza became president. Two years later, after Villa led a raid on Columbus, New Mexico, killing 16 Americans, Wilson sent troops under General John Joseph Pershing into Mexico to find the bandit. Carranza's government protested bitterly. Pershing failed to find Villa, who knew the territory well and had many supporters among its people, but the raid was a sign of the United States' readiness to use its "big stick" if necessary.

The U.S. and Latin America (1918–1939)

Many Americans were reluctant for the United States to become involved in World War I (1914–1918), seeing it as a European conflict. President Woodrow Wilson led the United States into the war in 1917, however, on the side of Britain, France, and their allies. Even before America's entry the conflict had provided a huge boost for the U.S. economy as production increased to meet the needs of the allies for foodstuffs, ships, and arms.

The end of the war in 1918 left the United States the world's dominant industrial economy. At the same time, the cost of the war in both money and casualties convinced many Americans to follow a course of isolation from international affairs. The United States, for example, refused to ratify membership of the League of Nations, the organization set up at the instigation of Woodrow Wilson to resolve international disputes by diplomatic means. It would soon become apparent that isolationism was hardly feasible for such a dominant power as the United States.

Changing status

The change in U.S. status was eventually to have a significant effect on the world economy but first affected Latin America. Britain had long been Latin America's biggest export market. South American commodities—minerals, coffee, and other foodstuffs—were traded for British industrial goods and loans. From the 1870s until 1914 the economies of Latin America had enjoyed sustained growth. Rising

LEFT: The United Fruit Company's hiring hall in Puerto Barrios, Guatemala, after it was captured by anticommunist forces in June 1954.

European demand for food and raw materials to supply its industries meant that the ruling elites of Argentina, Brazil, and Mexico fared well in a global free-trade environment in which tariffs were low. The doctrine of comparative advantage—inspired by 18th-century economist Adam Smith—held sway. It stated that countries would prosper by producing the goods they were best suited to make (*see* International trade and finance, page 35). With their tied, low-wage labor forces and plentiful land supplies Latin American businesses could undercut European competitors.

But world circumstances were changing. European families were falling in size, so the demand for Latin American goods fell too. Latin America produced so much food that world prices dropped, leaving commodity suppliers even worse off. Once the balance of economic power shifted to the western side of the Atlantic Ocean, the United States sold industrial goods to Latin America. Latin America paid with money earned from declining commodity and food exports to Europe. Meanwhile the United States would not import cereals, cotton, or sugar from Latin America because the government wished to protect the livelihoods of U.S. farmers who produced all these crops in abundance.

Economic imperialism in Latin America

In the 1920s U.S. enterprises quickly replaced old, established British businesses in Latin America, causing widespread local resentment. The British had concentrated their investment on utilities, infrastructure, and money-lending, building roads and railroads that ultimately benefited the indigenous population. By contrast, many U.S. firms exported commodities straight out of the country. As a result, a large share of potential Latin American exports—especially oil, minerals, and bananas—was now brought completely under U.S. control.

Such a process had been tried before. U.S. businesses had taken over sugar mills and plantations in Cuba in the 1890s. After 1918 the strategy became more systematic. In Chile the copper industry became completely controlled by subsidiaries of the U.S. Anaconda and Kennecott Corporations. In Bolivia U.S. companies acquired major stakes in tin-mining concerns, while Standard Oil took over several oil companies there and controlled the industry in Peru.

U.S. businesses took full advantage of weak Latin American governments that held little power on the world stage. They engineered generous tax breaks for themselves by employing local people at subsistence rates. The profits filled the coffers of the U.S. government and impeded the economic

LEFT: John Pierpoint Morgan (1837–1913), the powerful industrialist and financier who founded the bank J.P. Morgan & Co.

development of the Latin American countries from which the money had been derived. By the time the world entered the Great Depression of the 1930s, many Latin Americans saw the United States as a neoimperialist power whose only concern was the exploitation of the poor for its own benefit.

Fruit and banana republics

Over the last 100 years the banana has been the cause of bitter economic disputes between the United States, the nations of Central America, and more recently the European Union (EU). In 1870 bananas were unknown in the United States. By the end of the century U.S. citizens were eating 16 million bunches a year. The main force behind this development was Brooklyn-born businessman Minor Keith, who in 1871 built a railroad in Costa Rica, and whose ambition eventually led to him becoming the "Uncrowned King of Central America." Building railroads was, for Keith, part of a much bigger picture. He planted bananas on either side of the trackbed so that it became possible to transport them cheaply to markets in North America and Europe. Keith and his partners merged various companies and in 1899 founded the United Fruit Company (UFCO). It was the largest banana company in the world, with plantations in Colombia, Costa Rica, Cuba, Jamaica, Nicaragua, Panama, and Santo Domingo. Some countries relied on the trade so entirely that they became known by the derogatory name of banana republics.

The most important of UFCO's operations were in the Central American nation of Guatemala. The company received land and transportation concessions from the country's rulers, and Keith took advantage of what he called "an ideal investment climate" to buy land and build railroads. In 1901 the Guatemalan dictator, Manuela Estrada Cabrera, granted UFCO the exclusive right to transport mail between Guatemala and the United States. Before long Guatemala generated 25 percent of UFCO's total production, while UFCO controlled virtually all the country's transportation and communication. UFCO, for example, charged a tariff on all imports and exports that passed through the main port of Puerto Barrios. The country's coffee producers suffered because their prices became less competitive than those of other regions.

UFCO, Guatemala, and the CIA

The influence of UFCO pervaded Guatemalan life and commerce. The company was supported by the ruling right-wing dictatorship, which brutally suppressed uprisings by local people. Workers and opponents of the regime were terrorized, arrested, tortured, and killed.

In 1944 the people of Guatemala overthrew their right-wing dictator, Jorge Ubico. In its first ever elections the country elected Dr. Juan Jose Arevalo. Arevalo modeled his government on the New Deal policies that in the previous decade had helped the United States pull itself out of the Depression. In the following decade Guatemala put in place the roots of successful economic development, including more than 6,000 new schools and a progressive healthcare program.

Arevalo was succeeded by Jacobo Arbenz, who continued his predecessor's work and attempted to redistribute to the mainly Indian population unfarmed land that had previously been held by UFCO. UFCO pressed the U.S. government to complain about this redistribution of land. Protests in Washington ensued. President Dwight D. Eisenhower and Secretary of State John Foster Dulles warned that the "self-defense and self-preservation" of the United States were at stake unless what they termed "the Communist virus" was eradicated.

U.S. intelligence reports, widely publicized in the American media, described the situation in Guatemala as "adverse to U.S. interests" because of "Communist influence based on militant advocacy of socialist reforms and nationalistic policies." The Central Intelligence Agency (CIA) concluded that Guatemala was a Soviet satellite which threatened the security of the United States. A CIA memorandum also stated that Guatemala's policies "persecuted foreign economic interests, especially the United Fruit Company." The CIA carried

out a successful coup and replaced the democratic government with a right-wing dictatorship sympathetic to UFCO.

The influence of the U.S. government and UFCO had a lasting effect on Guatemala. Until recently the country was blighted by civil war and repression, and it is hard to avoid the conclusion that U.S. actions contributed to this situation. Although UFCO brought a sophisticated infrastructure and economic

TOP: The day the world changed: the front page of The New York Times *on October 30, 1929.*

ABOVE: Panic outside the New York Stock Exchange on October 29, 1929.

prosperity to the regions in which it traded, the prosperity never "trickled down" to the population as a whole.

In the 1970s the United Fruit Company changed its name to United Brands and ran into financial trouble. Eventually, its holdings were purchased by the Del Monte Corporation, which now operates in Central America in a less controversial fashion.

Between the world wars

Before the outbreak of World War I in 1914 the United States' main role in world trade had been as an exporter of agricultural and industrial products. The national economy was based on exports of food, raw materials, and technological innovations in machinery and engineering. Investment from European bankers meant that the United States was overall a debtor nation—meaning the value of its imports was greater than that of its exports—but this situation changed as U.S. overseas lending increased after the creation of the great banking dynasties founded by financiers like John Pierpoint Morgan and the Rockefeller family.

By the end of World War I in 1918 the United States had assumed a position of influence by becoming a creditor nation, a country that exported goods and services worth more than those it imported. During the 1920s U.S. loans to Europe helped the financial reconstruction of that war-ravaged continent. The U.S. dollar joined the British pound sterling and the French franc as one of the key reserve

currencies in the Gold Standard, an economic tool that set values by which international currencies were compared and traded.

By the end of the 1920s the United States had become the world's leading exporter and its second largest importer. Nevertheless, its foreign trade sector was still relatively small compared with its economy as a whole. This was because the U.S. economy—unlike the economies of France, Germany, or Britain—was virtually self-sufficient, being able to produce most of the goods demanded by its own population. While self-sufficiency improved the United States' standing in the world, it created problems for countries that owed money to the United States because they could not pay off their debts by trading.

The Wall Street Crash

The situation reached crisis following the meteoric rise in the Wall Street stock market during the 1920s. Instead of lending money to overseas nations, banks invested in more profitable stocks and shares at home. When Wall Street share prices crashed, the ensuing depression left the United States unable to afford imports from the rest of the world. To compensate, it soon refused to accept goods from overseas. Protectionism was codified in 1930 by the Hawley-Smoot Tariff Bill, which raised the prices of imported goods into the United States. Its effect was to bring international trade to a virtual standstill, and the Depression worsened because of it. Britain and other countries introduced similar legislation of their own.

ABOVE: *In New York in the 1930s, in the depths of the Depression, unemployed men form a line outside a charitable organization to get food for themselves and their families.*

In the early 1930s, partly as a result of the U.S. Exchange System by which the government restricted the outflow of gold from the country to boost its reserves, many countries abandoned the Gold Standard. World currencies fluctuated violently as a result. Although President Franklin D. Roosevelt tried to stabilize the situation by passing the Reciprocal Trade Agreement Act of 1934, which aimed to reduce tariff barriers and stimulate trade, in most other nations the prevailing mood remained predisposed toward protectionism.

Roosevelt also tried to regularize U.S. relations with Latin America by adopting what he called a Good Neighbor policy. He committed the United States to noninterference in the economic affairs of other countries. Perhaps the most significant result of the policy came in 1938, when the Mexican government nationalized the U.S.-controlled oil industry. Roosevelt refused to intervene.

U.S. insistence on high tariffs to protect its domestic industries contributed to the worldwide slump of the 1930s. The disastrous impact on Europe in particular created the conditions of social disintegration that fostered political extremism. In Germany the Nazis, who had been growing in popularity throughout the late 1920s, took power in 1933 when Adolf Hitler became chancellor.

The role of tariff barriers

The Constitution of the United States empowers Congress "to regulate commerce with foreign nations." This authority includes the right to impose import tariffs, taxes placed on products when they are moved from one country to another. Although tariffs raise money for the governments that impose them, their main purpose is usually to protect the industry of a particular country. This means they may be placed on imported goods at such a high level that people often will not buy them. Tariffs, otherwise known as import duties, made up half of all U.S. government income by the end of the 19th century.

In *The Wealth of Nations*, published in 1776, Scottish-born economist Adam Smith argued that world governments should adopt a laissez-faire approach to world trade. This meant that governments should provide very little or no protection to industries and agricultural firms, leaving the most efficient to thrive. The first sign that Smith was being heard came in 1846, when the British government repealed the Corn Laws that had restricted grain imports for centuries and protected British farmers from foreign competition. This allowed British consumers to buy cheap American grain. Gradually, the United States dropped many of its own tariff barriers and became a world trading nation.

Rebuilding postwar Europe

With a death toll around 20 million, World War II (1939–1945) was one of the most destructive conflicts in history. The Soviet Union bore the brunt of fatalities, losing some 12 million combatants and civilians in the conflict. Large expanses of Western Europe were obliterated by bombing, destroying the infrastructure that supported services such as transportation, communications, sanitation, and distribution. The vast numbers of European homeless urgently needed a massive house-building program.

One of the most devastated countries was Japan, whose attack on U.S. navy ships at Pearl Harbor in 1941 had brought the United States into what until then had been mainly a European war. In order to bring the war to a quick conclusion, the United States exploded two atomic bombs over the Japanese cities of Hiroshima and Nagasaki in August 1945.

The continental United States, however, was never seriously threatened with attack during World War II. Not only did it emerge unscathed; the devastation of Europe and the Allies' demand for equipment and supplies during the conflict provided a great boost for

ABOVE: An aerial view of the mushroom cloud from the atomic blast over Hiroshima, Japan on August 6, 1945. The United States used nuclear weapons to bring a swift end to World War II.

the American economy. Roosevelt's lend-lease scheme provided extended credit to allow the European nations to buy more than they could afford on the promise to pay it later. The economic growth caused by the war finally ended the Depression. The economic dominance of the United States, already the richest country in the world when the war began, was now unassailable.

A new world order

After 1945 the United States led the world into a period of sustained economic development that marked a radical departure from its previous emphasis on political and economic isolationism. Little of the resulting global prosperity would have been possible without the commitment of the United States. Without it the national interests of individual national interests would have pulled in too many different directions and rendered concerted action impossible. The United States' determination and ability to make the largest financial contributions to reconstruction and to lead the way in the creation of new world institutions gave it the ability to express its views forcefully and be taken seriously.

Part of the impulse behind the U.S. re-engagement with the rest of the world was the need for the United States to restore stability to the international situation by promoting economic recovery. Another impulse was that the postwar world offered an irresistible opportunity for U.S. business. The most important inspiration, however, was the expansionism of the communist Soviet Union in Eastern Europe. U.S. policymakers perceived that expansion as a threat to the economic and political well-being of the United States and determined to protect its values in any country under threat.

Bretton Woods

By 1944 it had become clear that the Allies—including the United States, the United Kingdom, France, Italy, and the Soviet Union—would defeat the Axis powers of Germany, Italy, and Japan. The liberation of countries occupied by the Nazis in Europe was already under way when the Allies began to develop plans for world economic reform.

These plans were sealed at the Bretton Woods Conference in New Hampshire in 1944. Delegates agreed on the establishment of three important new institutions: the International Monetary Fund (IMF), the International Trade Organization (ITO), and the International Bank for Reconstruction and Development (IBRD), the last of which has become commonly known as the World Bank (*see* International economic organizations, page 93).

The Iron Curtain and the Cold War

None of the proposed institutions could come into operation immediately after the end of the war as the Allies had intended. The Soviet Union took control of those countries of Eastern Europe it had liberated at the end of the war and began creating a series of communist satellite states ideologically and practically separated from their neighbors in the West. British Prime Minister Winston Churchill called the division that split Europe an "iron curtain." In the 1960s the barrier took on concrete form in the Berlin Wall, a fortified barrier between the communist and western sections of the German capital. Although the Iron Curtain was ostensibly intended to protect the Eastern bloc against military invasion, the real reason for its construction was to prevent economic and social contact between the two opposed ideological systems.

The period from the mid 1940s to 1989 is known as the Cold War, marked by immense distrust and mutual fear between the United States and the Soviet Union. The presumption that each was bent on world domination at the other's expense formed the chief backdrop to global political and economic relations, and saw the United States taking action overseas from Latin America to Southeast Asia.

The Cold War spurred U.S. determination to lead the world economy. Politicians in Washington, D.C., saw it as their duty to maintain and support a free and prosperous Europe as a buffer against Soviet expansionism. The strategy was aided by the fact that Western Europe had been so devastated by World War II that it was a ready market for cut-price U.S. goods: the economic rejuvenation of Western Europe would thus foster the conditions for renewed U.S. prosperity.

The IMF and foreign exchange controls

When it came into existence in 1947, the IMF attempted to end the previous decade's spate of currency devaluations. When a country devalues its currency, it makes its goods cheaper to export. Now U.S. influence on the IMF argued that that all currencies should be fixed in order to foster a degree of security and facilitate effective long-term planning.

The IMF determined the levels at which currency rates should be fixed, how they should be maintained, and when they should be changed. Significantly, the value of all currencies had to be fixed either in relation to gold or against the U.S. dollar. Immediately after the war, however, few goods were being produced other than by U.S. manufacturers. Trade was therefore limited, and countries needed to borrow U.S. dollars to pay for American goods, creating what was known as the "dollar gap."

The United Kingdom, exhausted by the war effort, refused to allow the pound sterling to be traded after 1945. At the United States' insistence it lifted those exchange controls in 1947 and found the pound had lost value against the U.S. dollar. The Bank of England tried to bail the country out but lacked the reserves to do so. The U.S. currency was unquestionably the strongest in the world.

The Marshall Plan

In March 1947 U.S. Secretary of State George C. Marshall, a former soldier, returned from a reparations conference in Moscow convinced that the European economies were in a disastrous state and that the Soviet Union wanted

to take advantage of this situation. The previous winter had been one of the bitterest in decades, worsening Europe's harsh economic plight. Food was rationed; shortages of coal, electricity, and steel plagued victors and defeated alike; many workers lacked the skills required for modern factories and offices, often because they had spent the greater part of the previous decade in the armed forces rather than learning a trade. There was widespread emigration from Europe, notably to North America, Australia, and Palestine.

In a speech at Harvard University in June 1947 Marshall outlined a plan for a European Recovery Program (ERP) to be administered by the Organization for European Economic Cooperation (OEEC) from Paris, France. The U.S. Congress, though initially wary of the plan, became increasingly convinced of the need for a "European bulwark" against communism. Although the ERP, commonly known as the Marshall Plan, had its roots in

ABOVE: General George C. Marshall (1880–1959), U.S. Chief of Staff during World War II and after it the initiator of the economic reconstruction plan that now bears his name.

opposition to the spread of communism, the Soviet Union was invited to participate. Joseph Stalin refused on behalf of the Soviet Union and all the other countries of the eastern bloc.

The ERP lasted 45 months and distributed more than $13 billion, equivalent to 1.2 percent of the United States' gross national product (GNP). The program produced spectacular results. Europe's GNP rose from $119.6 billion in 1947 to $159 billion in 1951, an increase of 32 percent. Such growth raised living standards in Western Europe and helped curb the spread of communism. The plan was a forerunner of later European economic integration in the European Union (EU).

European economic integration

Along with economic aid the United States supported closer ties among the European countries themselves. Again the move promised to strengthen the bulwark against

communism. When Britain made preferential trade agreements with Australia, New Zealand, and other members of the Commonwealth, on the other hand, the United States objected vigorously. Such agreements played little part in protecting the capitalist world.

In May 1950 French foreign minister Robert Schuman proposed that the production of French and West German coal and steel be placed under a common authority. Other European nations would be free to join this organization, the Coal and Steel Community. By making the agreement, France and West Germany—historically and traditionally bitter enemies—turned their backs on centuries of conflict. This was partly because they were both suffering severe aftereffects of World War II, and partly because both realized that world power had shifted away from them toward the United States and the Soviet Union, leaving cooperation as the only way for Europe to maintain its prestige.

The European Coal and Steel Community treaty was signed in 1951 by six nations: France, West Germany, Italy, and the Benelux countries (Belgium, Luxembourg, and the Netherlands). They became the founders of the European Union. Even closer integration between the Six, as the countries were often known, was achieved on the signature of the Treaty of Rome in 1957. It created a "common market," a free-trade region with a single tariff on imports from outside. Five years later the six nations devised a Common Agricultural Policy (CAP) that used a series of subsidies to allow European farmers to undercut their U.S. counterparts. This was not welcomed by the United States, and the CAP has been a matter of controversy at trade talks ever since.

Europe was still not unified. The United Kingdom, which had declined to join the Common Market, set up a competing European Free Trade Association (EFTA). It was joined by Austria, Denmark, Norway, Portugal, Sweden, and Switzerland.

The OEEC had achieved its goal of European recovery, but the United States felt that a similar organization was still needed to prevent trading discrimination. The United States also wanted prosperous European countries to join it in granting aid to developing countries. To this end it created the Organization for Economic Cooperation and Development (OECD).

The birth of GATT

The International Trade Organization (ITO) proposed at Bretton Woods was never successful. Partly because of its own tendency toward isolationism, the United States, although as vociferous a proponent of free trade in the late 20th century as it had been protectionist during the Depression, refused to ratify the new organization. The need for ITO was reduced, however, by the General Agreement on Tariffs and Trade (GATT),

ABOVE: The safety of beef for human consumption has become a matter of controversy at international trade negotiations.

BELOW: Six European nations sign the original European Common Market agreement (the Treaty of Rome) on March 25, 1957.

concluded by 23 countries in Havana, Cuba, in 1948. GATT, which evolved for the rest of the 20th century in various rounds of talks, laid down the conditions that govern world trade.

The first GATT round of talks set out the principles of multilateral and nondiscriminatory trade, and agreed that quantitative trade controls, by which states limited the amount of imports by imposing quotas, should be outlawed. GATT liberalized trade by preventing any preferential trading agreements designed to favor one nation over another. Consequently, the United States criticized the United Kingdom for its preferential trade agreements with Commonwealth countries that had formerly been part of its empire. Five years after the first agreement 34 countries signed up for GATT, accounting for 80 percent of world trade. GATT meant that by the mid-1950s U.S. import duties were 50 percent below their 1934 levels.

Latin America and the Cold War

During World War II many Latin American states supported the United States against the Axis powers of Germany, Italy, and Japan. The main exception was Argentina, whose leader Juan Perón sympathized with Nazi Germany and Fascist Italy. Although Argentina remained technically neutral, its predisposition toward the Axis meant that it missed out on postwar U.S. financial aid. This caused severe problems for Argentina's economy.

After 1945 U.S. dealings with South America were overshadowed by the Cold War and U.S. preoccupations with combating what it saw as the worldwide Soviet menace. The United States abandoned the "good neighbor" policy, fostered by U.S. President Franklin D. Roosevelt in the 1930s, and turned again to the "big stick diplomacy" that had characterized its relations with its neighbors in the first decade of the century. The combination of diplomacy and intimidation emerged whenever it appeared that the Soviet Union was trying to use local communist movements to further expansionism. The U.S. government was particularly hostile to left-wing movements in its own backyard in Central and Latin America, as it had been to the popular government of Guatemala in 1954.

When Fidel Castro overthrew the Cuban dictator Fulgencio Batista in the late 1950s, the United States became hostile to the island after he tried to implement an economic policy perceived by Americans as being against U.S. interests. In 1961 Castro proclaimed himself a Marxist and an ally of the Soviet Union. Alarmed, the United States imposed an

ABOVE: The United States has long taken a keen interest in bananas—not only in the fruit itself, but also in the countries that export it.

economic blockade on Cuba to strangle its economy. Even after the collapse of Soviet communism after 1989, U.S. sanctions against Cuba remained in place.

In 1965 the United States occupied the Dominican Republic to suppress a revolution that broke out in protest when conservatives overthrew the elected government. The following year U.S.-sponsored elections returned a conservative government to power. In 1983, when the pro-Soviet People's Revolutionary Government of Grenada was overthrown from within its own ranks, U.S. troops invaded the island and occupied it until 1985.

In the late 1970s U.S. President Jimmy Carter, in a change of U.S. policy, withdrew financial and military aid from the Nicaraguan dictator Anastasio Somoza. The weakened regime was overthrown by the socialist Sandinistas, whose government became a target of U.S. hostility. Carter's successor, Ronald Reagan, funded the training of counterrevolutionary Contra guerrilla forces that aimed to

overthrow the Sandinista government. A U.S. economic blockade on the country resulted in food shortages and hyperinflation.

The Alliance for Progress

There were also attempts to establish a more constructive relationship between the United States and Latin America. In 1961 President John F. Kennedy devised the Alliance for Progress, intended to avert further Cuban-style revolutions by promoting packages of social reform and economic development in Latin America. The main way it aimed to achieve this was through channeling U.S. money to anticommunist Latin American countries that were trying to industrialize. Although most countries in the area benefited in some way from the initiative, nevertheless by 1970 the Alliance for Progress had failed, mainly because the governments of Latin America, on the whole, failed to command sufficient authority within their countries to implement economic change.

ABOVE: More than a quarter of a century after the United States toppled the Chilean government of Salvador Allende, his memory was kept alive by opponents of Augusto Pinochet, the general who usurped him.

U.S. influence in Allende's Chile

In Chile socialist leader Salvador Allende won power in 1970 and headed a democratically elected left-of-center coalition government. His victory ended years of right-wing government in the South American state, but to the United States the result was a nightmare. It was already engaged in a war in Vietnam, and the last thing it needed was another country "going communist." There were many U.S. businesses in Chile, and Americans feared that the government might be nationalized by Allende without compensation to the foreign owners.

The United States attempted to destabilize Allende's government by withdrawing credits and economic aid to the country. The Chilean economy was ruined, with inflation at one point reaching 180 per cent. It is suspected that the U.S. Central Intelligence Agency stirred up internal discontent until, in 1973, Allende was deposed and killed in a military coup led by General Augusto Pinochet, who formed a right-wing junta and ruled the country himself. Pinochet, despite the atrocities he committed on his people, enjoyed the support of the United States and the United Kingdom. Both nations were grateful to have in place a leader who shared their anticommunist stance and could be relied on to protect foreign investment and preserve the status quo.

The Vietnam War

The Cold War tension that shaped American involvement in Latin America also framed its military involvement in Southeast Asia, where the defeat of Vietnam's French colonial government in 1954 left the country split into two, North Vietnam and South Vietnam. The United States supported South Vietnam against the communist North and in the early 1960s, as the North waged a terrorist campaign against the South, gradually increased the numbers of U.S. service personnel in Vietnam. From 1965 the United States was involved in a continuous war against the communists. In 1968 there were some 541,000 U.S. troops in the country; despite their presence, however, a successful communist offensive persuaded the U.S. government to reduce its troop numbers and leave the fighting to the South Vietnamese, although U.S. aircraft still carried out bombing raids on neighboring Laos and Cambodia.

By the time President Richard Nixon agreed the final withdrawal of U.S. troops in January 1973, nearly 60,000 Americans had died in Vietnam. Vietnamese casualties on both sides included more than a million military personnel and 415,000 civilians.

A rough estimate places the cost of the war to the United States at $150 billion, without including indirect or ongoing costs such

LEFT: Left-wing Sandinista supporters demonstrate outside the U.S. embassy in Managua, Nicaragua.

as payments to veterans. The impact on the U.S. economy was immense. Supporting the cost of the war severely limited President Lyndon Johnson's efforts to create his "Great Society" by diverting money from domestic programs. In 1966 and 1967 urban poverty boiled over into riots in a number of cities, including Los Angeles, Chicago, Newark, and Detroit. In January 1968 Johnson called for a 10 percent rise in income tax to pay for unemployment relief and the $25 billion annual cost of the war. When Richard Nixon became president in January 1969, his inaugural speech described America as "rich in goods but ragged in spirit."

The 1970s oil crisis

U.S. recovery in the 1970s was handicapped by events in the Middle East. For the United States the region was of vital economic importance as the source of the vast majority of the world's oil. The region was politically unstable, however, partly because of the existence since 1948 of the Jewish state of Israel, which was hated by virtually every Arab country. After an initial period of suspicion of the new state's socialist leanings the United States had come to support Israel for a variety of reasons, including the domestic political influence of Jewish Americans.

For years the leading oil countries, which were Arab, had kept prices down. In 1971 they increased them. Virtually overnight the United States was spending more on imports than it was earning from exports. Nixon tried to deal with inflationary pressure by cutting government spending and imposing a 90-day freeze on prices, wages, and rents. The policy led to "stagflation," a combination of rising prices and increased unemployment.

With the United States committed to substantial military spending in Vietnam and elsewhere, its gold reserves and currency plummeted. At the end of the year, facing a $5 billion negative balance of trade, the United States pulled out of the international currency system established at Bretton Woods and devalued the dollar to increase foreign exports. The move introduced a new period of economic uncertainty for Europe and the rest of the world.

Nixon's budget for 1973 set a deficit of $25.5 billion, the largest in U.S. history. In October 1973, however, the situation worsened when the Yom Kippur War broke out between Israel and its Arab neighbors. The Arab nations embargoed exports to the United States, western Europe, and Japan in retaliation for their support of Israel. The industrialized world entered a period of crisis (*see* box, page 77).

The United States and China

Some of the first signs of a thawing in the tension of the Cold War came in the early 1970s, when President Nixon opened a dialogue with Mao Zedong, veteran leader of communist China. The United States had a history of trade with China dating back to the 19th century but had backed China's Nationalists against Mao's communists in the long struggle for control of China. When the communists came to power in 1949, the United States recognized the exiled nationalist administration in Taiwan as the legitimate government of China. Now Nixon set out to woo China as an ally to reinforce his defense against the Soviet Union. In 1972 he visited China, and both countries announced a move toward normal relations that culminated in 1979 with full U.S. diplomatic recognition of China. The limited trading relations of the 1970s have today grown to the extent that the United States has

ABOVE: U.S. President John F. Kennedy (second from left) at talks with Soviet leader Nikita Khrushchev (right) in Vienna, Austria.

awarded China the status of most-favored nation, meaning that it enjoys the most beneficial trade conditions granted by the United States to trading partners..

By the end of the 20th century China had begun to embrace free-market principles and ran up the second largest national trade surplus with the United States, $19 billion. The main reason for the imbalance was that although China welcomed new export opportunities, it refused to take U.S. imports. In retaliation the United States imposed economic sanctions on the most populous country in the world, and Congress threatened to remove China's most-favored-nation status. The resulting uncertainty meant that U.S. business missed out on the huge infrastructure projects implemented all over the People's Republic of China in the late 1990s.

There were signs that the situation might be about to change. The United States had been anxious to open up what could be the biggest consumer market in the world. Despite concern in Washington, D.C., about Beijing's human rights record, China was granted fully fledged trading nation status. If rapprochement continues, the 21st century could see China becoming a real force in the world economy.

Trade wars

Every 10 years a new round of GATT talks takes place to discuss problems and possible tariff reductions. Its work is overseen by the World Trade Organization (WTO), established in 1993 after the slow and tense Uruguay Round of GATT trade talks, which were held up by disputes over agricultural subsidies. The WTO integrates all GATT talks into a single legal framework.

For all its successes, GATT has not brought unbroken harmony to international trade. The economic priorities of different regions still causes clashes of opinion that are sometimes described as trade wars. The most recent high-profile cases—including beef and bananas—have involved trade bodies authorized by the WTO.

The heaviest artillery in world trade wars, however, belongs to the United States. To the fury of its trading partners the United States has sometimes taken unilateral action to ban imports, most recently of Japanese steel. The most potent weapon in the U.S. armory is "Super 301" (*see* box, page 26), a provision of the 1974 Trade Act that authorizes U.S. government investigation not just of particular goods but also of the trading practices of a whole country. "Super 301" was originally formulated to prevent cheap Japanese goods from flooding into the United States.

ABOVE: Richard M. Nixon, the president who responded to the 1970s oil crisis by taking the U.S. dollar off the gold standard.

Another battleground

At the round of world trade talks held in Seattle, Washington, in November 1999 the key battleground was agricultural subsidies, which are of particular concern to Australia, Canada, and the United States. The United States, which is the world's largest agricultural exporter, urged "a coalition of support" for the abolition of export subsidies and the promotion of free trade in agriculture in the early part of the 21st century. Both the European Union and Japan resisted further demands for trade liberalization because they wanted to protect their agriculture, however. Environmental campaigners and others also staged often violent protests, arguing that liberalization would effectively enable western nations to exploit developing countries.

The European Union continues to voice criticism of U.S. export subsidies and state support of agricultural trade bodies. In the meantime, Australia, Canada, and the United States maintain that Europe subsidizes its farmers through the Common Agricultural Policy, now a $200-million subsidy paid directly to farmers. The EU is also preparing itself for further battles in the World Trade Organization over food safety standards. Within the EU there are conflicts among member countries about issues such as the safety of British beef, which other nations feared was infected with BSE, the so-called mad-cow disease.

The EU has already been involved in disputes with the United States over imports of hormone-treated beef, and there is growing public resistance in Europe to imports of genetically modified (GM) food. The EU hopes to use the next round of world trade talks to change the rules regarding health and safety in food. This threatens to lead to a bitter battle with the United States, which believes EU health fears to be groundless and appears committed to resisting international calls for limiting GM food production.

Why so much is at stake

The European Union and the United States are the two largest economies in the world today. Together the United States and the countries of the EU turn over around $1 billion a day and account for almost 40 percent of all world trade. Any joint decisions made by these two

ABOVE: *Ecological activists in Oxfordshire, England, protest genetic engineering by pulling up genetically modified crops.*

Super 301

"Super 301" is the name given to the section of the U.S. Trade Act that gives power to the U.S. Trade Representative to investigate countries to see if they grant fair and open access to U.S. exporters. Countries that fail the investigation are potentially subject to huge penalties. Under the terms of Super 301 anything that is considered to be an unfair practice by a foreign country can be stopped. Super 301 regulations aim particularly at preventing the sale of foreign goods to American companies at significant discounts, a practice that, if left unchecked, might cause the U.S. market to become flooded with cheap or subsidized foreign goods.

Recently, the worldwide steel industry has been investigated under Super 301 provisions partly because the strong dollar allowed producers from Brazil, Japan, and Russia to capture a large share of the U.S. market. Politics played a huge part in Super 301's reactivation. As the U.S. trade deficit with the rest of the world grew, Congress mounted pressure to protect U.S. industry from the rest of the world. The power of the protectionist lobby within U.S. government generally increases as an election looms.

economic superpowers—and, perhaps more significantly, any substantial disagreements between them—are bound to have profound repercussions on their other trading partners and the world market as a whole.

Overseas workers in the United States

Immigration has long been both a cause and an effect of U.S. economic wealth. The more workers exploit the country's immense natural resources, the more others see it as a land of opportunity. It is therefore a magnet for immigrants. Since the late 19th century the United States has been the most desirable destination for people seeking a new life in a country offering opportunities and the potential for an attractive lifestyle. For most of the 20th century the United States had the highest standard of living in the world. At century's end two-thirds of American families owned their own homes, and the United States

boasted more students than any other country. There were more business startups in the United States than in any other country.

The nation's motto is *E pluribus unum*—out of many, one. Apart from Native Americans, every citizen of the modern United States comes from an immigrant family. Approximately 80 percent of Americans are of European descent, and 12 percent are descended from blacks transported from Africa to work on plantations and build the railroad network. The rest are immigrants, predominantly from China, Japan, Mexico, the Philippines, Puerto Rico, Southeast Asia, and the Middle East.

The effect of slavery

The loss of large numbers of workers to the United States has had a significant effect on the economies of the nations from which there have been high levels of emigration. In some cases this is a cause of resentment, particularly in the case of slavery. The impact of the transatlantic slave trade on the economy of West Africa, for example, is difficult to quantify but is certainly profound. Perhaps the biggest effect has been what historians have termed "the psychological rape" of those countries that had 20 million of their population removed. In this sense the demands of the U.S. economy for a labor force to work its cotton plantations had a fundamental—and, many people believe, a detrimental—influence on the subsequent history and development of Africa.

Migration from Latin America

The United States' relatively poor neighbors in Latin America have long been the source of economic migration. Migration to the United States from Puerto Rico increased dramatically almost as soon as the United States took control of the Caribbean island from Spain in 1898. U.S. influence has transformed the island from an agricultural to an industrial economy. Today 17 percent of all pharmaceuticals sold in the world are made in Puerto Rico. Its resulting association with the Central American oil industry has made Puerto Rico the most polluted island in the Caribbean.

Mexican migrant workers started coming to the United States to work the cotton harvests after the American Civil War ended in 1865. By the end of World War I large numbers of Mexicans were working on large farms in the Central Valley of California. In World War II the United States lost many of its native workers to the military, creating a severe labor shortage. In July 1942 the U.S. and Mexican governments negotiated the Mexican Farm Labor Supply Program, known to most people as the bracero, the Spanish for "day worker," which allowed Mexicans to enter the United States for seasonal agricultural labor. The program benefited U.S. employers, while the government of Mexico believed the program helped its national economy because the braceros sent money from the United States to their families back in Mexico. When the program was terminated in 1964, illegal workers continued to flood from Mexico into the United States.

ABOVE: A migrant Mexican field worker's shack on the edge of a pea field in Imperial Valley, California. This photograph was taken in 1937.

Today major U.S. employers are in desperate need of overseas workers. The rate of unemployment in America is low compared with that of other countries, and the labor pool is shrinking. U.S. employers are now recruiting foreign workers with scientific, technological, and other specialized skills to help keep them dominant. A high proportion of today's U.S. workforce in leading edge, hi-tech industries is immigrants. More than half the computer science doctorates in the United States are awarded to foreign-born students.

America's new immigrants are also making major contributions to U.S. business with ideas and investment. Overseas managers help forge closer export links with their native countries. Meeting the United States' desperate need for skilled employees has a cost to the countries from which immigrants come. In the United Kingdom, for example, there is currently a skill shortage in the information technology sector because of economic migration to the United States. The economic cost to countries that lose workers to the United States will remain a matter of controversy well into the 21st century.

World debt

The United States is one of the world's major creditor nations, meaning that through international organizations and banks it is owed millions of dollars by other countries. This makes the nation an important player in the resolution of one of the world's most pressing economic problems, international debt. Countries in the developing world owe huge amounts to foreign creditors: Brazil, for example, owed more than $179 million in 1997.

Many of the debts date from the period since World War II, when many developing nations attempted to change their economies from agriculture to industry, which was apparently more profitable. They often placed high tariffs on overseas goods to prevent imports and protect their own new industries. This so-called import-substituting industrialization policy required huge financial intervention from the state. In the 1960s the world demand for commodities was strong enough to support this financial intervention. In the 1970s, however, when demand slackened, nations had to take out foreign loans to pay for it.

In the developed world banks built up huge reserves of deposits made by oil-rich nations whose wealth leaped following oil price rises during the early 1970s. The banks wanted to get good returns on loans and found that developing countries were hungry for money to fuel development. In the 1970s Latin American, Asian, and African nations took out loans totaling more than $500 billion.

In August 1982 Mexico announced that it was unable to repay the interest on its foreign

ABOVE: President Bill Clinton, who in 1999 appeared to support the cancelation of the developing world's debt to the United States.

LEFT: U.S. President Ronald Reagan and British Prime Minister Margaret Thatcher. In the 1980s the strict monetary control imposed by their governments had a major effect on many countries throughout the world by slowing down international trade.

loans; shortly afterward several other debtor nations made the same admission. The immediate cause of Mexico's interest default was a steep rise in U.S. interest rates after 1979, itself a consequence of the monetarist policies of U.S. President Ronald Reagan. The U.S. government restricted the supply of money and credit, forcing up interest rates and choking worldwide demand for goods. The problem for debtor nations was exacerbated when money markets withdrew their investments in those countries whose currencies were unable to meet their outstanding debts.

Structural adjustment policies (SAPs)

Debtor countries needed to take out further loans to pay their existing debts. Under the influence of the United States the International Monetary Fund (IMF), which administered the new loans, made it a condition that countries put in place austerity budgets, also known as structural adjustment policies (SAPs). SAPs forced developing countries to adopt market economy disciplines in order to qualify for new loans. Typically, this meant drastically reducing public spending and increasing interest rates to reduce inflationary tendencies. State enterprises were privatized, forcing up prices and unemployment, and sometimes leading to social disorder. As living standards fell, the governments of countries such as Colombia, Pakistan, and Peru started to turn increasingly blind eyes to domestic producers of illegal drugs. The drug trade appeared to be the only way in which these countries could generate enough revenue to survive. As a result the western world was soon flooded with unprecedented quantities of cocaine and

heroin. The drugs rapidly found their way to the markets where they would earn the most money. Top of the list was the United States, and the consequent damage to U.S. society has been immense.

Since the late 1970s about 30 African countries have adopted SAPs with the approval of both the IMF and the World Bank. Many of the poorest sub-Saharan nations have been unable to transform their economies by these methods, however. Ethiopia, Rwanda, and Sudan have seen their foreign debt more than double between 1982 and 1990, reaching a combined total of $164 billion. In the industrialized world it became increasingly clear that there was little to be gained from continuing to charge these countries interest on debts that could never be repaid in full. This realization increased the pressure on the principal lenders, especially the United States and the countries of the EU, to find a new and radical solution to an otherwise intractable problem.

The cancelation of world debt

A proposal that could turn out to have a profound effect on the world economy was made in September 1999 by U.S. President Bill

Clinton. Clinton, approaching the end of his final term of office and perhaps anxious to ensure a place in history, offered for the first time to write off 100 percent of the world's debt to the United States. In an address to a joint session of the IMF and the World Bank Clinton said that the United States, then enjoying an unprecedented boom, had a "moral imperative" to make a greater effort to help relieve the poorest countries of billions of dollars of debt by the start of the new millennium. Clinton urged Congress to respond to his request for $970 million to close the funding gap for the so-called highly indebted poor countries (HIPC) initiative and said the United States was ready to give a further $1 billion to wipe out all outstanding debts of this type.

Despite Bill Clinton's support, it was doubtful whether the initiative would be passed through the Republican-dominated Congress. During the Clinton presidency Congress moved toward a more isolationist stance that echoes earlier U.S. attitudes to foreign affairs. For example, Congress repeatedly refused to pass legislation that would make the United States pay the $1 billion it owes to the United Nations.

ABOVE: *President Richard M. Nixon shaking hands with with Chinese leader Mao Zedong. The two politicians did much to reestablish some of the United States' long-lapsed trading links with China.*

Clinton's intervention was made partly in the hope of ensuring that savings made on loan repayments to the United States would be spent by poor countries on domestic health-care and education measures. The president was also attempting to create a situation in which at least some of the 38 countries currently classified as "developing" could be admitted into world trade talks in order to get them more integrated into global commerce.

Contemporary issues

As the most powerful economy in the world, the United States has far more complex effects on other countries than simply through trade negotiations or initiatives to cancel debt. Some of the major ways in which U.S. influence is felt on the world scale are the effects of its fiscal and monetary policies, its attitudes to environmental issues, the strength of its arms industry, and its attitudes toward human rights in other countries.

The U.S. Federal Reserve

The United States' role in the world economy depends not only on the U.S. government but also on the Federal Reserve, or Fed, the central banking system that controls the U.S. economy. The Fed board is responsible for approving discounts and other rates of interest, supervising foreign business, and generally regulating the operation of all banking systems. The Fed's tight monetary policies have been impressively effective in controling inflation, and the independence of its decision-making has been widely admired. In the United Kingdom, for example, the structure of the Fed was partly copied in 1997 when Prime Minister Tony Blair separated the Bank of England from the Treasury.

Although many people would argue that the president of the United States is the most powerful person on the planet, there is a strong case for saying that whoever heads the Fed has more power and influence than any other figure. The Fed chairman is appointed for a term of four years, allowing each president to put in place his own nominee. He or she controls interest rates in the United States. Because the United States is the world's biggest consumer of goods, raising or lowering U.S. interest rates often moves currencies on the world's markets. Moves by the Fed can

ABOVE: Demonstrators gathered outside the Rio Earth Summit to remind the diplomats taking part of the high stakes for which they were playing.

also change economic policies in countries around the world, affecting the employment prospects of a workforce.

Alan Greenspan, chairman of the Fed since 1988, has gotten much of the credit for the longest boom in U.S. history. It was Greenspan's decision to raise U.S. interest rates in the summer of 1998 that many pundits believe averted a world economic crisis. During that summer Russia defaulted on its loans from the International Monetary Fund, while Brazil, Japan, and countries in Southeast Asia found themselves in severe economic difficulties that caused hardship to millions of people. Foreign currency speculators caused currencies in those countries to plummet by selling them at a furious rate. By raising U.S. interest rates, Greenspan made it easier for countries to trade with the United States, which in turn helped them out of recession.

Environmental issues

The United States is an active participant in the international campaign to clean up the earth in the interests of preserving the eco-system. Many critics still believe that it is not yet active enough. A wide range of environmental concerns was brought into sharp focus at the United Nations Conference on Environment and Development (UNCED), held in Rio de Janeiro, Brazil, in June 1992. More than 100 world leaders attended the emergency summit aimed at protecting the earth's well-being. At Rio the industrialized nations assumed responsibility for a global ecological crisis that threatens irreversible climate changes and environmental disaster unless human behavior is altered. Many environmentalists fear that the planet is entering an era in which hurricanes, tornadoes, and floods caused by rising sea levels will sweep the earth. Measures to limit environmental damage included reducing automobile exhaust emissions, restricting the burning of fossil fuels, and slowing the destruction of the rain forests.

In 1997 the United States and other industrial countries signed a treaty in Kyoto, Japan, committing all nations to reducing the emissions of greenhouse gases, which trap the sun's heat in the atmosphere, causing temperatures to rise, to below 1990 levels. The U.S. Senate has so far failed to ratify this treaty. In fact the rate at which the United States releases carbon dioxide and other gases into the atmosphere is accelerating.

ABOVE: Peasants armed with sticks and stones try to stop themselves being evicted from occupied land by Guatemalan police. Some people believe the U.S. government should apply more economic pressure to aid environmentalist and humanitarian movements.

The Kyoto treaty will impose significant costs on the United States, and this explains the U.S. government's reluctance to reach the targets it set. To achieve them, energy prices will have to rise in order to dissuade people from using their cars. The United States is attracting worldwide pressure to raise its gasoline prices, which are very low by international standards. The average price for a gallon of gas is five times cheaper in the United States than in the United Kingdom, for example. Cheap gas prices encourage greater use of the car, which in turn hinders the chances of the United States meeting the commitment to the environment it made at the Kyoto summit.

U.S. legislators face a problem. In no other country in the world is the car such a symbol of personal freedom as it is in the United States. Since 1970 the U.S. population has increased by 33 percent, but the number of cars on the road has risen by 100 percent. It is one of the problems of the democratic system that politicians facing reelection find such issues difficult to deal with.

The global arms trade

Another important way in which the United States influences the economics and politics of the world is through the sale of arms and munitions. The ending of the Cold War and the collapse of communism after 1989 added many new names to the list of countries with which the United States was prepared to trade weapons. Before 1990 the U.S. government would sanction the sale of arms only to its closest allies; but now that there is no longer an ideological struggle between western capitalism and Soviet communism, U.S. arms have been made much more widely available. The country leads the world in total arms-trading agreements, both for the modification of existing weapons systems and delivery of new ones. Military manufacturing companies such as McDonell Douglas have a close relationship with the federal government. Arms sales generate substantial overseas funds and tax revenues.

The arms industry gives the United States the power to support or not support certain countries or regimes. Long after the end of the

LEFT: Although developed countries were united against Saddam Hussein, elsewhere there was opposition to war in Iraq. Here the U.S. flag is desecrated by demonstrators in Casablanca, Morocco.

Cold War, for example, the United States caused international controversy by continuing to supply weapons and military training to the forces of Chile's right-wing dictator, General Augusto Pinochet. Although widely reviled by liberal opinion, Pinochet was seen by the United States as someone who could prevent the spread of communism in South America. In India and Pakistan, meanwhile, the United States has chosen to sell arms to both countries despite the tension between them focused on the disputed province of Kashmir. U.S. policy is that it would be dangerous for either side to become significantly better armed than its neighbor.

U.S. dominance of the arms trade and the volatile nature of some regions of the world mean that it is entirely possible that one day U.S. weapons will be used against U.S. troops. In the Persian Gulf War of 1989, for example, the United States and its allies launched air and ground strikes to drive the Iraqi troops of Saddam Hussein out of Kuwait, which they had occupied shortly before. Previously, however, the United States had actually supported Saddam during the war between Iraq and its neighbor, Iran.

Human rights issues and trade sanctions

In the same way as the U.S. government has a flexible policy mandate when it comes to supplying arms to various countries, it is also flexible on the question of trade sanctions against countries that are guilty of violating human rights. As with the sale of weapons, there does not seem to be any rigid code governing these sanctions: decisions to impose them are based on economic and political expediency. Critics of U.S. links with China, for example, believe that the United States could make more use of its influence to force the Chinese to reconsider human rights issues such as the judicial process and the treatment of political dissidents.

Economic sanctions—generally, bans on the purchase and sale of oil—have become an important tool of U.S. foreign policy. Under U.S. influence, for example, many western nations have banned various types of trade with nations including Serbia and Iraq.

These boycotts can lead to a wide range of economic problems and have often caused the governments of other countries to question the wisdom of U.S. policy. Economic dominance, they argue, does not give the United States either a monopoly on wisdom or moral superiority. The United States, whose isolationist tendencies have made it something of a reluctant superpower, is still learning to be comfortable in its role as the world's only superpower. The complex relationship between economic interest, political expediency, and morality continues to be a puzzle.

LEFT: Oil wells went on burning in Kuwait City long after the end of the 1990 Gulf War.

International trade and finance

In this chapter we look at the history of world trade and examine how it is structured and how it works, using practical examples of familiar everyday goods.

International trade occurs because, through it, each country or region of the world can enjoy greater production, consumption, and—ultimately—economic welfare than if there were no trade at all. If there is full employment of all factors of production—land, labor, capital, and entrepreneurship—a country can increase its production of one good or service by diverting resources away from the production of other goods. If resources are scarce, but a country concentrates these scarce resources and factors of production on producing the goods it makes best—that is, those for which it is most efficient—total world production can thereby be increased.

Clearly, therefore, gains from specialization and trade are possible if countries can agree to exchange that part of their output which is surplus to their own needs. Thus, for example, South Africa, which has the world's largest reserves of diamonds, will use as many of these precious stones as it needs and then either sell the remainder to other countries for profit or else exchange them for different goods of the same value. Countries with highly developed techniques of mass production will sell the goods produced by these methods to nations with less advanced infrastructures.

ABOVE: This painting of a harbor market in Italy reflects the growth of trade in the 18th century.

BELOW: The widespread availability of computer technology has been one of the main driving forces in the growth of modern trade.

Early trade

For many years international trade—and with it the "internationalization" or "globalization" of much of the world's economy—has been largely taken for granted. Today it is difficult to imagine a world without trading blocs, international trading agreements, quotas, international borrowing, and other arrangements intended to facilitate trade.

However, it is important to remember that the development of international trade has been a gradual process that has sometimes been opposed, and that has not been entirely free from setbacks.

Indeed, although there have been major advances in the growth of international trade (particularly during the 18th and 19th centuries and since the end of World War II in 1945), impediments to the expansion of trade have occurred, especially during the early part of the 20th century, when a great many protectionist measures

Trade wars in the 1990s

As the world's largest economy, the United States is the most powerful adversary any nation can face in a trade war. One of the most formidable weapons at the United States' disposal is "Super 301," a provision of its 1974 Trade Act that authorizes the investigation of particular goods and the trading practices of an entire country.

If countries are found not to be granting fair and open access to U.S. exporters, they are liable to huge penalties. Super 301 was originally designed for use against Japan, but the provisions of the act were suspended when the United States joined the World Trade Organization (WTO) in 1995. However, in March 1999 President Bill Clinton reactivated Super 301 in the context of growing trade tensions between the United States and other nations, especially those of the European Union (EU).

ABOVE: If banana-producing nations can no longer rely on their main export as a source of revenue, there may be severe political repercussions.

Banana wars

Between 1993 and 1999 the U.S. authorities were increasingly in conflict with the EU over a range of European products, which eventually came to include French cheese and Scottish cashmere sweaters. At the center of the dispute was the claim by the United States that European import rules favored bananas from their former Caribbean colonies over those from Central American companies. The controversy arose after the introduction in 1993 by the EU of a new banana-import policy. These regulations protected the former colonies of Britain and France by waiving trade tariffs on their banana trade with Europe and giving them guaranteed quotas. The EU argued that without such preferential treatment, the banana industry in the Caribbean would collapse and jobs would be lost. Meanwhile, however, Latin American banana growers faced tariffs on their exports to the EU and received no quota guarantees.

This incensed the United States, which responded to the EU move by threatening to impose huge tariffs on a range of European goods that would have made them uncompetitive in the U.S. market. Although the World Trade Organization ruled in April

1999 that the EU banana import regime was out of line with international trading rules, they did not uphold the demands made by the United States for retaliatory sanctions of $500 million, so there was no clear victor in the banana wars.

Steel clashes and beef battles

The devaluation of the Asian currencies in 1998 led to a flood of cheap steel into world markets. When Japanese steel exports to the United States surged by 400 percent in 1998, closely followed by large exports from Korea, Brazil, and Russia, the U.S. Congress began a rallying cry for protection of its own steel industry. It was estimated that 10,000 jobs in U.S. steel plants were lost in the wake of this export surge.

Although the United States reached agreements with Brazil and Russia on voluntary reductions in steel shipments, Japan refused to cut back production, claiming that it was not its fault if the U.S. steel industry could not compete internationally. In April 1999 the U.S. Commerce Department ruled that Japan had violated trade laws and proposed tariffs of up to 67 percent, although the U.S. Senate refused in June 1999 to pass a bill imposing these quotas.

In 1999 the EU refused to allow American hormone-treated beef into Europe because of fears that the growth hormones in the meat might cause cancer, nerve disorders, and other health problems. This was an argument that the United States vigorously rejected, stating that Europe should comply with a World Trade Organization ruling and accept imports of U.S. beef. The United States held that the European action amounted to protectionism, and U.S. trade officials published a detailed list of European products worth more than $900 million that they threatened with 100 percent punitive tariffs unless the EU backed down. In response the EU pointed out that in 1989 the United States had promised to export only hormone-free beef to Europe because of the EU's ban.

Despite the offer from European trade negotiators to pay compensation to U.S. farmers (who were claiming $500 million for lost business) and allow North American producers better access to other markets, the U.S. government maintained that only tariffs would force the Europeans to change their minds.

Other trade disputes

U.S. trade wars in 1999 were not confined to bananas, beef, and steel. In April of that year the United States filed seven complaints with the WTO against Argentina, Canada, the EU, India, and South Korea. These complaints were about manufacturing, agriculture, intellectual property rights, and government procurement.

In July 1999 a major trade row broke out between the United States and Australia and New Zealand over lamb imports. U.S. President Clinton announced that he was going to limit lamb imports to 1998 levels and impose a 40 percent tariff on any additional imports in order to protect U.S. sheep farmers. Australia reacted by cutting taxes for its own lamb producers in order to cushion the blow.

LEFT: The U.S. dollar is more than just a national currency—it is one of the most dependable assets in the world.

were implemented by the Western industrial nations as they sought to shelter their domestic industries from economic depression and increased competition from newly industrialized countries. While since 1945 many institutions have been set up that are designed to facilitate the smooth functioning of trade, the late 1990s were a time when the threat of trade wars increased, bringing a greatly increased likelihood of damage to the world economy (*see* box on page 36).

The growth of money

When people talk about an "international monetary system," they are basically referring to the conditions under which different national currencies are exchanged for each other in order to settle the claims and debts arising from foreign trade and other international financial transactions. Like trade, the general acceptability of international money has been a gradual development.

Primitive bartering

The earliest known form of trade was barter, a system in which goods are exchanged for each other. Bartering is usually carried out by societies in which no single good has come to play a special role, and in which no object has acquired a symbolic value in the way that money has in modern society. Although widely practiced by primitive peoples, barter was a severely limiting and inconvenient form of exchange: if, for example, one trader had a cow and wanted to trade it for a camel, he had to find someone who had a camel and wanted a cow. The exchange was further complicated if one item was clearly more valuable than the other.

Thus it came about that at a very early stage in such transactions within a given society, some particular commodity, or commodities, would become widely acceptable as a common medium of exchange. If these commodities were not needed for immediate consumption by the person who accepted them, he or she would be able to store them for consumption at a later time or for future use in purchasing some other commodity. This medium of exchange is what we now know as "money."

Although different early human societies used different goods as money, a few metals—primarily silver and gold—and an alloy—brass—came to dominate the monetary scene because they were easier to use and more stable in value than any other material. Silver and gold later superseded brass as the basic form of money because these metals were generally agreed to have the same intrinsic value the world over. This remained true even though the very fact that they were used as money tended to boost their values far above the amounts that they would have commanded as mere commodities. The acceptability of gold and silver was not affected by national borders—everyone knew their worth, and they were thus the first truly international currencies.

The case for trade

We begin our look at international trade by considering some theory and seeing how the market forces operating in a perfectly competitive market economy can (subject to various assumptions) achieve a state of economic efficiency. Within an isolated and relatively small economy markets may be too small to be competitive, and monopoly may predominate. One of the benefits of international competition and trade is that they are likely to make markets more competitive and therefore more efficient.

Adam Smith recognized this in the 18th century, and it was he who first drew attention to the benefits of division of labor in the context of workers specializing in different productive tasks within a factory that itself was specializing in a particular type of product. Smith extended the discussion to an analysis of the specialization between regions and countries. He demonstrated why there was—and should be—division of labor not only within a single plant but also among plants within a firm, among firms within an industry, among industries within a country and even among countries!

If a country specializes in producing the goods in which it is already most efficient, a large scale of production may allow it to benefit in two ways—from increasing returns to scale and from economies of scale. A return to scale is defined as the proportionate increase in output that results from proportionate increases in all inputs. Economies of scale are factors that cause the average cost of producing a commodity to fall as output of the commodity rises—for example, if a firm can double the number of items it produces without doubling its costs, it has achieved an economy of scale.

Industries within that country then become even more efficient when long production runs—i.e., greater numbers of units produced—allow firms to introduce more advanced machinery and improved technology. Without international trade the limited extent of the domestic market may prevent a country from benefiting fully from economies of scale. International trade and specialization extend the market available to firms and businesses, and so allow the full benefits of the division of labor and economies of scale to be achieved.

Absolute and comparative advantages

If a country can produce a particular output of a good or service at the lowest cost in terms of resources used, the country is deemed to be efficient in terms of technique and productivity in producing the good. If a country is better at, or more technically efficient than, other countries in producing a good or service, it is said to possess an absolute advantage in that good's production. If the country is not the best at what it does, it suffers from an absolute disadvantage when compared with other, more technically efficient producers. A country enjoys a comparative advantage in the production of a good if that good can be produced at lower cost when compared to other goods the country produces.

To illustrate both absolute advantage and comparative advantage, consider the following example of the "world" economy—which is highly simplified, based on the assumption

BELOW: In addition to the normal range of goods that you might expect to find in a street market, some stalls in Rio de Janeiro, Brazil, also sell foreign currency.

	Timber (units)	Cotton (units)
United States	36	18
United Kingdom	9	18
"World" total	45	36

Table 1 U.S./U.K. two-commodity trade example (initial position)

	Timber (units)	Cotton (units)
United States	72	0
United Kingdom	0	56
"World" total	72	36

Table 2 U.S./U.K. two-commodity trade example (after specialization)

that there are just two countries, the United States and the United Kingdom, with two units of resource (man-years of labor and machines, for example), and that they produce just two commodities, timber and cotton. We also need to make four other assumptions. First, that factors of production are totally mobile within each country and that they can be instantly switched between industries (although in real life such factors are very immobile between countries, even though final goods and services can be traded). Second, that there are constant returns to scale and constant average costs of production in both industries in both countries. Third, that both the commodities produced, cotton and timber, are in demand in both countries. And fourth, that the limited resources and factors of production in each country are fully employed.

Suppose that each country has equal resources and devotes one half of its resources to timber production and the other half to cotton. The production totals are as given in Table 1, above. The United States possesses an absolute advantage in both industries. While it is four times as efficient in timber production, it is as efficient in cotton production as the United Kingdom. If the United Kingdom produces an extra unit of cotton, it need give up only half a unit of timber. By contrast, the United States must give up two units of timber in order to increase production of cotton by one unit. So while the United States has an absolute advantage in both commodities, it possesses a comparative advantage in timber production, whereas the United Kingdom (with an absolute disadvantage in timber) has a comparative advantage in cotton production.

If each country then specializes completely in the activity in which it possesses a comparative advantage, the production totals are as shown in Table 2. Although there is now a gain of 27 units of timber, there is no gain in units of cotton. If at least as much of one good and more of the other results from specialization and trade, a welfare gain has occurred.

Terms of trade

The rate at which timber is exchanged for cotton—in other words, the ratio at which a country can trade domestic products for imported products—is known as the "terms of trade." Economic theory shows that if export prices rise more quickly or fall more slowly than import prices, an improvement in the terms of trade will follow.

Where the United States has an absolute advantage in the production of both goods in our example, that country will be prepared to give up no more than two units of timber for one unit of cotton, whereas the United Kingdom will require at least half a unit of a timber for one unit of cotton if trade is to be worthwhile. The terms of trade in this example lie between half a unit of timber and two units of timber for one unit of cotton, the exact rate of exchange being determined by the strength of demand.

In the real world, however, millions of goods and services are traded all the time, and to measure a nation's average terms of trade, economists use index numbers. The average prices of exports and imports are calculated using weighted indexes, and the export index is divided by the import index to give the terms-of-trade index. A rise in the index shows an improvement in a nation's terms of trade, indicating that a given quantity of exports now pays for more imports than before.

Exchange rates

We already know that trade can result in gains to both the parties involved—indeed, that is the main reason for its existence. We will now examine why that should be the case.

It is important to consider how trade actually occurs. In the real world private households, corporations, banks, and governments buy and sell goods and services every day from and to countries all over the world.

Before any transaction takes place, and depending on where the individual household or firm is situated, a currency swap will probably be made between the two parties. If an individual living in Pennsylvania, for example, wishes to buy a cotton shirt (made by a British firm) from a dealer in Boston, Massachusetts, then the transaction will take place in U.S. dollars. However, workers at the British company that made the shirt receive their salaries in pounds sterling. Clearly, somewhere between the buyer of the shirt and its producer a currency exchange must have been made.

The amount of goods and services that are bought and sold internationally depends in part on the rate of exchange. The exchange rate is the ratio at which two currencies are traded on the foreign exchange market. Our final piece of theoretical analysis needs to consider the impact of exchange rates on

BELOW: Much of the cotton harvested from this field in Arizona will be sold in the domestic U.S. market, but a significant proportion of it will be sold abroad.

	Timber (per foot)	Cotton (per bale)
United States	$1	$2
United Kingdom	£3	£4

Table 3 U.S./U.K. two-commodity trade example (prices).

trade in our two-country model outlined above. Consider again the example of a "world" economy that comprises just two countries, the United States and the United Kingdom, producing just two commodities, timber and cotton. The current prices of both goods for domestic buyers is as set out in Table 3, above.

If U.S. and U.K. buyers have the option of either buying at home or importing goods to meet their needs, their choice will depend on the exchange rate. Starting with the assumption that the exchange rate is at par ($1 = £1), from the perspective of the U.S. buyer it is apparent that neither British timber nor cotton is competitive at this rate. A dollar will buy a foot of timber in the United States but only one-third of a foot if it was converted into a pound sterling. The price of British timber to an American is $3 because it will take $3 to buy the necessary £3. Similarly, $2 buys one bale of cotton in the United States, but the same $2 buys only half a bale of British cotton. The price of British cotton to an American is $4, twice the price of the domestic product.

At this exchange rate, therefore, the British find that U.S.-produced timber and cotton are less expensive than timber and cotton produced in the United Kingdom. Timber at home in Britain costs £3, but £3 buys $3, which buys three times as much timber in the United States. Similarly, cotton costs £4 at home, but £4 buys $4, which buys twice as much U.S.-made cotton. With an exchange rate of $1 = £1, the United Kingdom will import timber and cotton, and the United States will import nothing.

Assume now that the exchange rate is £1 = $0.25 or, in other words, that the price of a pound is $0.25. A dollar will now buy £4. At this exchange rate the British buy timber and cotton at home, and the Americans import both goods. Under the new exchange rate Americans must pay a dollar for a foot of U.S. timber, but the same amount of timber can be bought in Britain for $0.75 (remember, £1 costs $0.25, so £3 must cost $0.75). Likewise, cotton that costs $2 per bale in the United States costs Americans half as much as in Britain because $2 buys £8, which is the price of two bales of British cotton. The British are not interested in importing because both goods can be purchased more cheaply at home than abroad. Now the United States imports both goods, and Britain imports nothing.

With our examples so far, trade flows entirely in one direction or the other. What happens if that exchange rate changes again, so that $1 = £2 (or £1 = $0.50)? First, the British will buy timber in the United States because British timber costs £3 per foot, but £3 will buy $1.50, which gets one and a half feet of U.S. timber. Buyers in the United States will find British timber too expensive, but Britain will import timber from the United States. At the new exchange rate both sets of buyers will be indifferent to whether the cotton comes from Britain or the United States: to

ABOVE: The German firm Volkswagen is a leading foreign importer of automobiles into the United States. Here one of their Jetta models is unloaded from the cargo ship Frisia at Wilmington, Delaware.

U.S. buyers domestically produced cotton costs $2 but, because $2 buys £4, a bale of imported cotton also costs $2; and British buyers also find that cotton costs £4 regardless of whether it is domestically produced or imported from abroad. Thus there is likely to be no trade in cotton.

If the exchange rate changes just slightly, so that $1 buys £2.10, there is a change in the trade patterns. Although U.S. timber is still cheaper to both Britons and Americans, British cotton begins to look good to U.S. buyers. Cotton produced in the United States costs $2 per bale, but $2 buys £4.20, which buys more than a bale in Britain. When $1 buys more than £2, trade begins to flow in both directions: the United Kingdom will import timber, and the United States will import cotton.

Factor endowments

What actually determines the sources of comparative advantage in a country? Quite simply, it is the "factor endowments"—the quantity and quality of labor, capital, land, and natural resources. Factor endowments—in particular natural resources, knowledge capital, physical capital, land, and skilled and unskilled labor—account for a large proportion of world trade patterns.

But comparative advantage is not the only reason that explains why countries trade. Countries both import and export similar goods and services, differentiating their products to suit different tastes. For instance, while the United States has a thriving automobile industry, some U.S. consumers are attracted to Japanese cars, often because they are more fuel-efficient and smaller than their U.S. rivals.

Even if the U.S. automobile industry responds and copies the style and design of the Japanese cars, there will still be some consumers who will not switch to smaller U.S.-produced cars—perhaps through force of habit or because of the good service that they have had from the Japanese supplier.

The growth of international trade

By the early 18th century Europe had become the world's dominant commercial force, accounting for 69 percent of all trade in 1720 and for 77 percent by 1800. This preeminence was achieved partly because Western Europe and its colonies in Africa, Asia, and Latin America were in a much better position than either the rest of Europe or Eastern civilizations to build up wealth (accumulate capital). Unprecedentedly high levels of trading were achieved partly through a great increase in the sheer volume of mercantile activities and partly because European powers now owned so many of the earth's natural resources. This prosperity created a slow but steady rise in incomes. To make the same point in economic terms, Europe had a favorable resource base, which meant that there was a margin above subsistence level that allowed this trading to take place.

In addition, it should be noted that there was at the time no social class in Asia, the Middle East, or for that matter in Eastern Europe that was comparable to the Western European bourgeoisie, which accumulated so much moveable wealth over such a long period.

ABOVE: The façade of the Customs House overlooking the Thames River in London, England. Much of that country's wealth has been derived from trade with foreign countries.

Such a process of accumulation was vitally important for the later exploitation of new technologies and the development of manufacturing processes, as well as for the modernization of agricultural equipment and techniques. It also provided the means to improve infrastructures and educational facilities. The European drive to accumulate capital, albeit often very slowly over many centuries, provides an important pointer to the long-run origins of trade development, emphasizing the essential continuity of that process as opposed to the concept of a dramatic structural break.

19th-century European expansion

Between 1815 and 1914 the total value of the world's international trade grew by 20 times in monetary terms during a period in which the world's population only doubled. Europe was chiefly responsible for this expansion: by 1913 the exchange of goods among European nations or between them and the inhabitants of other continents accounted for two-thirds of the world's trade. Throughout, Britain was the largest trader because of its growing need for imported foods and raw materials, its export of coal and manufactures, and its considerable entrepôt trade—i.e., trade that involved the storage, packaging, and distribution of goods that were ultimately destined for another country.

Britain's share of expanding trade declined as the commerce of other countries grew; yet by 1913 the country's overseas trade still comprised one-sixth of the world's total. Germany's rapid industrialization meant that by 1913 about one-eighth of the world's trade was either crossing its borders or passing through its ports. It was only the United States, outside the European bloc, that managed to encroach on this hold by Germany and Britain during World War I (1914-1918).

The growth of foreign trade increased greatly the dependence of many European economies on external buyers and sellers. In 1800 Britain could just about feed itself: by 1914, however, it was importing more than half of its foodstuffs; and for every dollar spent on imported food, drink, and tobacco, another dollar was spent on overseas raw material and 66 cents on manufactured goods. In return, Britain's biggest export was coal (it shipped abroad around one-third of its output), followed by 80 percent of its cotton output. Other major exports included iron and steel, engines, machines, chemicals, and steamships built for foreign buyers, along with books, clothes, crockery, shoes, and liquor. In all, these exports accounted for one-third of the country's total output from farms, mines, and factories. Germany's rapid industrial growth began to give its economy a similar overall composition, though with a smaller

ABOVE: A coal mine near Chesterfield, Derbyshire, England. For many years coal was the United Kingdom's prime source of energy and a major earner of foreign currency.

dependence on food imports. By 1913 about one-fifth of German production was exported. France meanwhile had managed to remain relatively self-sufficient—it was able to provide most of its domestic food and power requirements from within its own borders.

Britain was the only country to do more trade outside Europe than within. In 1914 British exports were divided almost equally between Europe (34 percent), the British Empire (37 percent), and foreign countries outside Europe (29 percent). Britain's five best customers were India, Germany, Australia, the United States, and France. The five chief markets in which it bought goods were the United States, Germany, India, France, and Argentina.

After 1815 London was the world's biggest exporter of financial capital, with loans and investment pouring out to continental Europe and beyond. The importance of this for the British economy was twofold. First, it enabled Britain for at least 75 years of the 19th century to finance developments abroad, such as the Indian railway system, also supplying engineers, iron, and rolling stock in an inclusive "package deal." Second, financial capital exports made possible the expansion of world trade, thus enabling foreign countries to borrow pounds sterling, many of which were used to buy British products. The contraction in the world's trade that took place in the years between the two world wars (1919–1939) led to the cessation of financial capital exports. This caused irreparable damage to the British economy and heralded the end of its period as a world power.

After the end of World War II in 1945 international trade resumed apace, and since 1950 it has grown 14 times, to be worth more than $6.5 trillion by 1997. In the same period the proportion of world economic output attributed to trade increased from 8 percent to 26 percent. Since 1945, however, critics have argued that this growth has been achieved unfairly at the expense of workers in poorer countries, who have been exploited. Rich countries have maintained protectionist policies, and poor countries have not enjoyed the benefits of free trade because they have not had the requisite manufacturing infrastructure.

ABOVE: The headquarters of National Panasonic, the electronics multinational, at Osaka, Japan.

The case for protectionism

The case for specialization in trade has been made through the theory of comparative advantage. This theory has shown that any country will gain in terms of increased production, efficiency, and welfare, provided that the goods it specializes in and trades cost less to produce than the goods it does not specialize in.

However, there is no guarantee that these gains will be distributed equally among trading nations. Although restrictions on free trade will reduce the well-being of many parts of the world, some countries—particularly the better off—might still feel that it is in their own best interests to impose such barriers; and governments actually do impose tariffs on a regular basis. There are several common arguments advanced in favor of these restric-

BELOW: Crop spraying in the county of Hereford and Worcester, England. Historically, the United Kingdom has been eager to protect its farmers against foreign competition.

A problem with protection

ABOVE: The U.S. government had to intervene on behalf of domestic computer manufacturers to counter the threat posed by cheap imports from Japan.

In July 1991 the U.S. government imposed a 62.7 percent tariff on imports of active-matrix liquid crystal display screens ("flat-panel displays"), which were used for laptop computers from Japan. The U.S. Commerce Department argued that Japanese producers were selling their screens in the U.S. market at a price below cost. Such a practice is known as "dumping"; and when it occurs, it can threaten the survival of domestic producers.

The United States responded by introducing a tariff to protect domestic producers of flat-panel screens. However, U.S. computer manufacturers knew that the U.S. laptop screens were of a lower quality than the displays made in Japan and recognized that if they used U.S. screens, it would be only a

matter of time before sales of their final product declined in the face of higher-quality competition from abroad. Rather than pay the tariff for the higher-quality screens from Japan, two of the big U.S. laptop producers—Apple and IBM—announced that they would move their production facilities abroad.

No good deal

In this instance the imposition of a tariff was more harmful than beneficial: American consumers and producers of laptops were hurt since they had to pay higher prices for laptops, costs of production escalated, and the U.S. flat-panel screen industry was hurt through the loss of buyers for its product.

tions to free trade, as we will see below. This policy—known as "protectionism"—might be approached in a number of different ways.

Protectionism defends infant industries

Protectionism is often used to defend young industries against attacks by established rivals in the same market. The policy may be of particular benefit when there is scope for the young industries to benefit from economies of scale. If, for example, a newly established industry in a developing country is unable to compete with firms in other countries that are already benefiting from economies of scale, protectionism may be justified, particularly

during the early growth stages. Some strategic trade theorists argue that comparative advantage is not necessarily the product of luck and history. They maintain that governments can use industrial policy—in the form of financial aid or subsidies—to invent or create comparative advantage for selected industries. Governments often have considerable discretion in these matters, although any action they may take almost invariably involves as much guesswork as sound economic rationality. However, as shown in the box above, the efforts made to protect the burgeoning "flat-panel display" industry in the United States during the early 1990s backfired considerably.

Dumping

Any commodity that is sold on a foreign market at a price below its marginal cost is said to have been dumped. Dumping may be in the interests of an exporting country that wants to eliminate competition and thereby gain a monopoly in the targeted foreign market. The country exporting a commodity or commodities on this basis may therefore support the short-run losses incurred by dumping to gain a later advantage. An exporting country may also dump in order to dispose of temporary surpluses and thus avoid reductions in the price of the commodity in the home market and loss of income by the producer.

How a dump is determined

The General Agreement on Tariffs and Trade (GATT) supports the imposition of special import duties to counteract dumping if it can be established that the practice is damaging a domestic industry. Dumping is prohibited under the terms of the Treaty of Rome, the foundation stone of the European Union.

Rules for all GATT member governments were originally agreed on as part of the round of talks that concluded in 1967 between North America, the EU, and the European Free-trade Association (EFTA). They were reviewed at the most recent Uruguay Round of GATT.

Dumping is a shady activity, and it is often difficult to prove or tell for certain if it is taking place. Nevertheless, it is easier to prove in a market economy, where the prices and input costs of products can be readily compared. For planned economies the EU compares the price of the product exported with that produced in a free-market, non-EU country. If such a free-market price cannot be determined, the EU judges a fair price on the basis of its own calculations of the costs of production.

The United States government must obtain the approval of the International Trade Commission before imposing antidumping duties on imports, and its decisions may still be overruled by the U.S. Court of International Trade.

ABOVE: The Hasbro factory at Pawtuckett, Rhode Island. Toy manufacture is one of the industries that may be adeversely affected by dumping.

Protectionism saves jobs

The model of comparative advantage assumes that all the factors of production—land, labor, capital, and entrepreneurship—are fully employed and perfectly mobile within countries. In the real world, however, if large-scale unemployment exists, a case can be made for using factors inefficiently rather than not employing them at all. It may, for example, cost society less to keep an unprofitable factory open than to close it if the workers cannot find alternative employment and cause yet more joblessness.

Complete freedom of trade may result in structural unemployment. This type of unemployment stems from the decline of industries that are unable to compete or adapt in the face of either changing demand or comparative cost and advantage. However, there is no reason to believe that the workers laid off in a contracting industry will not ultimately be reemployed in other expanding sectors. Consider the increased foreign competition in textiles, which resulted in thousands of U.S. textile workers in New England losing their jobs over the last 35 years of the 20th

century. The expansion of high-tech industries, however, led to the unemployment rate in Massachusetts falling to one of the lowest in the United States by the mid-1980s, and New Hampshire, Vermont, and Maine also experienced a boom in job creation. It was followed by further unemployment in New England in the early 1990s, as manufacturers of high-tech hardware moved their business abroad. By the mid-1990s, however, small and medium-sized U.S. companies began to create new jobs in sectors such as biotechnology and computer software.

Protectionism prevents unfair competition
It is sometimes claimed that low-wage countries in the developing world exploit local labor in order to produce cheap goods. Quite simply, the developing country has a comparative advantage because it is paying its workers low wages, and therefore the key component of its production costs is lower than it would be in an industrialized country. However, wages in a competitive economy reflect productivity: workers in the United

ABOVE: In the United States the growth of biotechnology compensated for job losses in other sectors.

LEFT: Tariffs applied to watches are particularly complex in the United States.

States or Germany, for example, earn higher wages than workers in comparable jobs in other nations because they are more productive. Trade also flows not according to absolute advantage but according to comparative advantage, and all countries benefit even if one country is more efficient at producing everything.

Methods of protection
A government that has adopted protectionism may implement its policy in a variety of ways—by tariffs, export subsidies, import quotas, export taxes, and "red-tape" barriers. They are discussed in detail below.

Tariffs
A tariff is a tax on imported goods. Generally, a tariff is any tax or fee collected by a government. There are two basic ways in which tariffs may be levied: specific tariffs and ad valorem tariffs. A specific tariff is levied as a fixed charge per unit of

Trade wars in the 1930s and the formation of GATT

When the Great Depression hit the United States in 1929, the U.S. government responded by dramatically increasing tariff rates in the Smoot-Hawley Tariff Act of 1930. The Smoot-Hawley Tariff Act raised tariffs to an average rate of 60 percent on many products imported into the United States. The intention was to protect U.S. businesses from foreign competition and so help reduce the growing unemployment rate. However, more than 60 U.S. trade partners around the world swiftly retaliated with higher tariffs of their own. The final effect was to reduce world trade in the 1930s to less than one-quarter of the level of trade that had occurred in the previous decade. Most economists now believe—and it quickly became obvious to many politicians at the time—that the higher tariffs of the time probably contributed to the depth and length of the Great Depression in the United States and elsewhere.

Security through trade

After World War II the United States and other Allied nations believed that trade restrictions were detrimental to world economic growth. The General Agreement on Tariffs and Trade (GATT) was therefore initiated to promote trade liberalization among its member countries. The method of GATT was to hold multilateral tariff reduction "rounds." At each round countries would agree to lower tariffs on imports by a certain average percentage in exchange for a reduction in tariffs by other countries of an equal percentage. Although GATT agreements never achieved a movement to free trade by all member countries, they did represent significant steps in that direction. Since the General Agreement came into operation in 1948, there have been eight rounds of negotiations, with progressively lower tariff rates by member nations. The last round of negotiations—the "Uruguay Round"—reduced existing tariffs by a third.

In a sense, then, the GATT represents an international cooperative agreement that facilitates movement toward the

ABOVE: *This man had been rich in the 1920s, but by 1931 he had been reduced by the Great Depression to selling apples on the sidewalk.*

free-trade strategy set for all countries. If a GATT member-nation refuses to reduce its tariffs, then other members would refuse to lower theirs. If a GATT member raises its tariffs on some product above the level that it had previously agreed, then the other member nations are allowed, under the General Agreement, to retaliate with increases in their own tariffs. In this way nations have a greater incentive to move in the direction of free trade and a disincentive to take advantage of others by unilaterally raising their tariffs.

ABOVE: *Many buildings in the United States became derelict during the Great Depression because their owners could not afford upkeep and maintenance.*

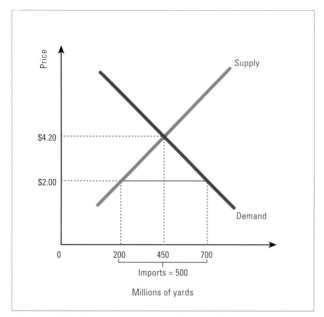

Figure 1 U.S. domestic supply and demand for cotton.

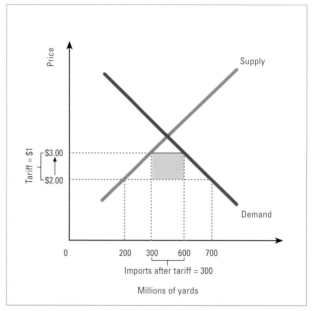

Figure 2 The effect of a $1/yard tariff on imported cotton.

imports. For example, the U.S. government levies a 5.1 percent specific tariff on every wristwatch imported into the United States. Thus, if 1,000 watches are imported, the U.S. government collects $51 in tariff revenue. In this case, $51 is collected whether the watch is a $40 Swatch or a $5,000 Rolex.

An ad valorem tariff is levied as a fixed percentage of the value of the commodity imported. Ad valorem is Latin for "in proportion to the value." The United States currently levies a 2.5 percent ad valorem tariff on imported automobiles—a levy that is justified as a means of protecting the domestic car industry in the United States. Thus if $100,000 worth of autos are imported, the U.S. government collects $2,500 in tariff revenue. In this instance $2,500 will be collected regardless of whether the vehicles imported are two $50,000 BMWs from Germany or ten $10,000 Hyundais from South Korea.

Sometimes both a specific and an ad valorem tariff may be levied on the same product simultaneously. This is known as a "two-part tariff." For example, wristwatches imported into the United States face the 5.1-cent specific tariff as well as a 6.25 percent ad valorem tariff on the case and the strap and a 5.3 percent ad valorem tariff on the battery.

Different tariffs are generally applied to different commodities. Governments rarely apply the same tariff to all goods and services imported into the country. One exception to this occurred in 1971, when President Richard Nixon, in a last-ditch effort to save the Bretton Woods system of fixed exchange rates (see page 93, International economic organizations), imposed a 10 percent ad valorem tariff

ABOVE: A consignment of Honda automobiles on a transporter. Each of these Japanese vehicles will probably be subjected to a tariff when they are exported to other countries.

on all imported goods from International Monetary Fund (IMF) member countries. But incidents such as this are uncommon.

Figures 1 and 2 on page 49 show how gains from trade might be lost by the imposition of a tariff.

Figure 1 shows domestic supply and demand for cotton. In the absence of trade the market will clear—i.e., demand will equal supply—at a price of $4.20. At equilibrium 450 yards of cotton are produced and consumed. Assume now that cotton is available at a world price of $2, the price in dollars that Americans must pay for cotton from foreign sources. If we assume that an unlimited amount of cotton is available at $2 and there is no difference in quality between domestic and foreign cotton, no domestic producer will be able to charge more than $2. If they do, U.S. consumers will simply buy foreign cotton. In the absence of trade barriers the world price sets the price in the United States.

As the price of cotton in the United States falls from $4.20 to $2, the quantity demanded by consumers increases from 450 million yards to 700 million yards, but the quantity supplied by domestic producers drops from

BELOW: This textile factory in North Carolina would be protected by the imposition of tariffs on cotton from outside the United States.

450 million yards to 200 million yards. The difference, 500 million yards, is the quantity of cotton imported.

Now suppose that the U.S. government is not happy with this situation because less cotton is being produced and sold domestically, and that it wishes to curb the amount of cotton imported. Figure 2 shows the effect of setting a tariff of $1 per yard on imported cotton, so as to reduce imports, and increase domestic supply and demand. The tariff raises the domestic price of cotton to $2 + $1 = $3. The result is that some of the gains from trade are lost. Consumers are forced to pay a higher price for the same good. The quantity of cotton demanded drops from 700 million yards under free trade to 600 million yards because some consumers are not willing to pay the higher price.

Simultaneously, the higher price of cotton attracts some marginal domestic producers who could not make a profit at $2 into cotton production. As the price rises to $3, the quantity supplied by producers rises from 200 million yards to 300 million yards, and the result is a decrease in imports from 500 million yards to 300 million yards.

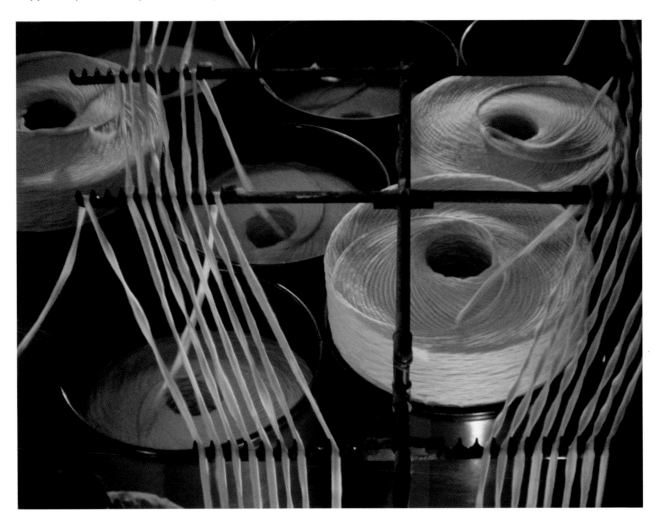

The shaded area in Figure 2 shows the revenue that the government collects: this shaded area is equal to the tariff rate per unit ($1) times the number of units imported after the tariff is in place (300 million yards). The receipts from the tariff are thus $300 million. While domestic producers receive a higher price and earn higher profits, the higher profits are achieved at the cost of a loss of efficiency. This is because domestic consumers have to pay a higher price for a reduced quantity of the product than they would have had to pay if there were no tariff.

In the early 1930s the world economy experienced a collapse in international trade and a trade war between nations as tariffs were imposed by governments. The box on page 48 examines trade wars in the 1930s.

Export subsidies

In certain circumstances a government may seek to help domestic producers by providing them with financial support that will enable them to compete in foreign markets with producers from abroad. This form of support is known as export subsidy. Financial assistance of this type will reduce the costs for exporters and distort trade by affecting the market price. As with taxes, subsidies can be levied on a specific or ad valorem basis.

Historically, the commodity groups to which export subsidies have most commonly been applied are agricultural and dairy products. There are several reasons for this. Agriculture has long been regarded as the bedrock of world economic prosperity, and—partly as a result of this preconception—the farmers in many countries have often held great political power. This has been particularly true in France, a country whose economic self-sufficiency was largely due to the productivity of its farms.

In order to maintain its traditional position, the farming sector within the European Union (EU) has always enjoyed high levels of subsidy. Farmers' incomes have been maintained by restricting domestic supply, raising domestic demand, or by a combination of both measures. One common method of protectionism is through the imposition of "price floors" on specific commodities, so that when there is excess supply at the lowest (floor) price, the EU must stand ready to purchase the surplus. These purchases are often stored for future distribution at a time when there is a shortfall of supply at the floor price. This is why the EC has a so-called Butter Mountain.

Sometimes the amount of produce that the EU must purchase exceeds its available storage capacity. When this happens, the EU must either build more storage facilities, at some cost, or devise an alternative method to dispose of the surplus inventory. It is in these situations, or in order to avoid these situations, that export subsidies are sometimes used. By encouraging exports, the EU can reduce the domestic supply and thus avoid the problems that may be caused by having to purchase the excess.

ABOVE: A rancher in Nebraska. The U.S. government is eager to support the activities of its farmers through the Export Enhancement Program (EEP).

In the United States one of the main export subsidy mechanisms is the Export Enhancement Program (EEP). Its stated purpose is to help U.S. farmers compete with farm products from other subsidizing countries, especially those in the EU. The EEP's major objectives are to challenge unfair trade practices, to expand U.S. agricultural exports, and to encourage the other countries that export agricultural commodities to undertake serious negotiations to resolve outstanding agricultural trade problems.

As a result of the commitments agreed as part of the GATT Uruguay Round negotiations in 1986, the United States has now established annual export subsidy quantity ceilings by commodity and maximum budgetary expenditures. In other words, it has set limits not only on the number of units that may be imported but also on the amount of money that may be spent on them. Commodities eligible under EEP initiatives are wheat, wheat flour, semolina, rice, frozen poultry, frozen pork, barley, barley malt, table eggs, and vegetable oil. In recent years the U.S. government has made annual outlays of over $1 billion on the EEP and its Dairy Export Incentive Program (DEIP). Meanwhile, the EU has competed by spending more than $4 billion a year to encourage exports of its own agricultural and dairy products.

Import quotas

Import quotas are another popular protectionist measure that limits the quantity of imports into a country during a specified period of time. An import quota is typically set below the free-trade level of imports—i.e., it allows less to be brought into the country than would have been imported if no limits existed. Restrictions of this type are known as "binding quotas."

If on the other hand a quota is set at or above the free-trade level of imports, then it is referred to as a "nonbinding quota." Goods that are illegal within a country effectively have a quota set equal to zero. Thus many countries have a zero quota on narcotics and other illicit drugs, which are all banned by law.

There are two basic types of import quota: absolute quotas and tariff-rate quotas. Absolute quotas limit the quantity of imports to a particular level during a specified period of time. Sometimes these quotas are set globally and thus affect all imports, while at other times they are set only against goods from particular countries. Absolute quotas are generally administered on a first-come-first-served basis. For this reason many quotas are filled shortly after the opening of the quota period. Tariff-rate quotas allow a specified quantity of goods to be imported at a reduced tariff rate during the specified quota period.

In the United States in 1996 milk, cream, brooms, ethyl alcohol, anchovies, tuna, olives, and durum wheat were subject to tariff-rate quotas. Other quotas exist on cotton, peanuts, sugar, and syrup. In the United States the administration of most quotas is carried out by the U.S. Customs Service, which monitors ports of entry to the country.

BELOW: Imported automobiles from Japan await loading onto freight trains at Richmond, California. From here they will be distributed across the United States.

Among the quotas that are not regulated by this body are those on dairy products (which are administered by the Department of Agriculture), watches (controlled by the Department of the Interior), and watch movements (which are under the aegis of the U.S. Commerce Department).

Mandatory quotas

The most severe and punitive quotas are mandatory quotas because they simply cut the volume of imports without involving foreign governments in the decision-making process. Voluntary quotas are milder, being negotiated between countries. One of the best-known examples of this type is the agreement between Japan and the United States in 1981 by which Japan agreed to reduce its automobile exports to the United States by 7.7 percent from its 1980 level. When this agreement came to an end in 1985, Japanese automobile imports into the United States jumped by over 70 percent. In the United States today quotas are currently imposed on a wide range of products, including color TVs, motorcycles, and mushrooms.

Export taxes

As its name suggests, an export tax is a tax collected on exported goods. As with tariffs, export taxes can be imposed on a specific or an ad valorem basis. In the United States export taxes are unlawful since the U.S. constitution contains a clause prohibiting their use. It was imposed because of the concerns of cotton producers in the southern states who exported much of their product to England and France. However, many other countries impose export taxes. To take just a few examples, Indonesia applies taxes on palm oil exports; Madagascar applies them on vanilla, coffee, pepper, and cloves; Russia uses export taxes on petroleum; and Brazil imposed a 40 percent export tax on sugar in 1996. In December 1995 the EU imposed a $32 per ton export tax on wheat.

"Red-tape" barriers

There are other trade policy mechanisms that governments will use to restrict imports. One of the more common is a "red-tape" barrier. It involves setting up a costly administrative procedure that is then made a requirement for the importation of foreign goods into a country.

Red-tape barriers can take many forms: France once required that video cassette recorders (VCRs) enter the country through one small port facility in the south of France. Because the port capacity was limited, it effectively restricted the number of VCRs that could enter the country. A red-tape barrier may also arise, for example, if multiple

ABOVE: Baling cotton in California. U.S. cotton is one of several agricultural commodities protected by import tariffs.

licenses must be obtained from a variety of government sources before importation of a product is allowed.

International institutions, trade blocs, and customs unions

For a variety of reasons it often makes sense for nations to coordinate their economic policies rather than act alone. Coordination can generate benefits that cannot be achieved through unilateral action. If countries cooperate and set zero tariffs against each other, then they are likely to benefit more than when they attempt to secure short-term advantages by setting tariffs.

Benefits may also accrue to countries that do any or all of the following in concert: liberalize labor and capital movements across borders; coordinate fiscal policies (e.g., taxes) and resource allocations toward agriculture and other sectors; coordinate their monetary policies (e.g., interest rates). Any type of arrangement in which countries agree to coordinate their trade, fiscal, or monetary policies is known as economic integration. There are several different degrees of integration.

Following the lengthy and damaging trade wars of the 1930s, the United States and 22 other nations initiated the GATT (see box on page 48), the principal aim of which was to prevent another breakdown in world trade similar to the one that had taken place during the runup to World War II. The GATT allowed the creation of free-trade areas (FTAs) and customs unions (CUs) between members; both these arrangements aimed to liberalize trade between members.

Free-trade areas

Every member of an FTA is allowed to determine its own trading policy with outsiders. An FTA is formed when a group of countries agrees to eliminate tariffs among themselves but at the same time maintains or imposes external tariffs on imports from the rest of the world. The North American Free-trade Area (NAFTA) is an example of an FTA. NAFTA was created in 1994 for an initial period of 15 years between Canada, Mexico, and the United States. When NAFTA is fully implemented, tariffs on automobile imports between the United States and Mexico will be zero, but Mexico will be permitted to continue to set a different tariff from the United States on automobile imports from non-NAFTA countries. Because of such different external tariffs FTAs

ABOVE: Import tariffs are a source of revenue for the government, but they do not necessarily stop people from buying foreign goods. The automobiles here at the Beverly Hills Hotel in California include a British Rolls Royce and a German Mercedes Benz.

generally develop elaborate "rules of origin." These rules are designed to prevent goods from being imported into the FTA member country with the lowest tariff and then trans-shipped to another country with higher tariffs. Of the thousands of pages of text that make up the NAFTA agreement, most of them describe rules of origin.

Customs unions

A customs union is typically characterized by a common external tariff. It restricts members' freedom of action and usually involves greater economic integration between members who adopt common policies in addition to the basic common external tariff. The EU is a prime example of such an arrangement. Although a customs union avoids the problem of developing complicated rules of origin, it introduces a new problem, that of policy coordination among the participating states. With a customs union all member countries must be able to agree on tariff rates across many different import industries. Such consensus is not always easy to achieve.

Common markets and economic unions

A common market is an agreement between two or more nations that establishes free trade in goods and services, sets common external tariffs among members, and also allows for the free mobility of capital and labor across countries. The leading example is the EU, which was established as a common market by the Treaty of Rome in 1957, although it took many years for the full transition to take place. Today EU citizens have a common passport, they can work in any EU member country, and can invest throughout the union without restriction.

An economic union will typically maintain free trade in goods and services, set common external tariffs among members, allow the free mobility of capital and labor, and also delegate various fiscal spending responsibilities to a supranational agency. The EU's Common Agriculture Policy is an example of fiscal coordination of a type that is characteristic and indicative of an economic union.

Trade agreements

A preferential trade agreement (PTA) is perhaps the weakest of all forms of economic integration. Countries participating in a PTA would generally offer tariff reductions, though perhaps not eliminations, to a set of partner countries in some product categories. Higher tariffs—which might perhaps be nondiscriminatory—would be kept on all remaining product categories.

This type of trade agreement is not allowed among World Trade Organization (WTO) members, which are obliged to grant "most-favored-nation" status to all other WTO members. Under this most-favored-nation (MFN) rule countries agree not to discriminate against other WTO member countries. Thus, if a country's tariff on bicycle imports, for example, is 5 percent, then it must charge 5 percent on imports from all other WTO members. Discrimination against, or preferential treatment for, some countries is not allowed under the terms of the agreement. The country is free to charge a higher tariff on imports from non-WTO members, however.

In 1998 the U.S. government proposed legislation to eliminate tariffs on imports from the nations in sub-Sahara Africa. This action represented a unilateral preferential trade agreement, since tariffs would be reduced in one direction but not the other.

The role of the U.S. dollar in international trade

Thus far we have looked at how trade occurs, some of the factors that determine trade, and the development of world trade since the 18th century. We have examined some of the arguments in favor of free trade and and those in favor of protectionism, and we have outlined the roles of international institutions, trade blocs, and customs unions in facilitating the process of trade.

Now we turn our attention to the U.S. dollar, the currency that has had a larger role than any other currency in the development of modern trade. This is because of its strength and stability over a long period and its consequent reliability as a hedge against erosion of value (inflation).

Since the early 1970s the development of the system of international finance has been influenced by two related sets of developments. First, the abandonment of the Bretton Woods system of fixed exchange rates in the early 1970s was followed by a movement to adopt floating exchange rates. This development—which was part of a growing belief in the need for markets to determine exchange rate movements—was brought about by a series of strains on the old system that arose from persistent U.S. balance-of-payments deficits (*see* box on pages 58-59).

Second, there was a gradual removal of restrictions on international capital flows, which allowed freer movement of capital across the globe. Taken together, these developments had important implications for the role of the U.S. dollar in international financial markets (*text continues page 60*).

BELOW: In November 1999 a U.S. trade delegation flew to Beijing in an attempt to thrash out the obstacles preventing China's admission to the World Trade Organization (WTO).

The World Trade Organization

ABOVE: *President Bill Clinton speaks at the 50th anniversary of GATT-WTO in Geneva, Switzerland, May 1998.*

The 50 years after the end of World War II in 1945 saw enormous growth in international trade. Merchandise exports increased by 6 percent on average annually throughout this period; total trade became 14 times greater than it had been in 1950. Much of the credit for these great advances in prosperity went to the General Agreement on Tariffs and Trade (GATT).

The need for closer links

By 1995 the governments taking part in GATT decided that the time had come for the formation of a new body that would facilitate closer trade links and help trade flow more smoothly, freely, and fairly from country to country. To this end the World Trade Organization was set up in Geneva, Switzerland, in 1995 as a development of GATT. There are currently 135 members, who account for 90 percent of world trade.

Closer relations have also resulted in more detailed and complex negotiations. In February 1997 WTO reached a historic agreement on telecommunications services, with 69 governments signing wide-ranging liberalization measures that went far beyond those agreed in the final Uruguay Round of GATT. In the same year 40 WTO governments successfully concluded negotiations for tariff-free trade in information technology (IT) products, and 70 members concluded a financial services deal covering more than 95 percent of trade in banking. At the ministerial conference in Geneva in May 1998 WTO members agreed to study the trade issues arising from global electronic commerce.

The WTO is further charged with the development and policing of multilateral trading agreements along the principles followed by the eight rounds of trade negotiations concluded under GATT.

Balance of payments

ABOVE: *British coins. The United Kingdom has been forced to devalue its currency, the pound sterling, on a number of occasions when facing a persistent balance-of-payments deficit.*

A nation's international balance of payments is a reflection of its total commercial and financial transactions with all other countries of the world. It is, in effect, a balance sheet that records all incoming and outgoing payments over a given period. In theory a nation's balance of payments is like a double-entry bookkeeping ledger—it should always be in equilibrium, and the total saved and earned should be exactly the same as the amount spent and loaned.

In practice, however, that balance is almost never achieved. If a country has a trade deficit, its outgoings are greater than its incomings. If, on the other hand, a nation has a balance-of-payments surplus, it earns and receives more from export trade than it spends abroad. This is not good because that country's surplus is made at the expense of another country's deficit.

For accounting purposes a country's balance of payments is generally listed in three categories: current account, capital movements, and reserve settlements.

Current account
A nation's current account includes the balance of trade, which is a record of all payments for imported and exported merchandise. Other items listed in the current account are payments for services (such as shipping costs and insurance), money spent abroad by private citizens, and dividends and interest on foreign investment. Finally, it also includes payments made to the country by foreign governments and international organizations. Among such payments are those for economic and military assistance to foreign countries and for the maintenance of military forces stationed abroad. It should be noted that government grants are sometimes listed under the heading capital movements (see below).

Capital movements
In simple terms capital movements are a list of a country's savings and borrowings. When they appear in a balance-of-payments account, they reflect the amount of domestic capital invested abroad by private individuals, firms, and the government (including both short-term and long-term investments), and of foreign capital received from abroad.

Reserve settlements
Reserve settlements register any additions to or subtractions from the country's monetary reserves that result from all transactions listed in the two previous categories. They include gold settlements, International Monetary Fund transactions in regular and special drawing rights, and changes in foreign exchange assets.

U.S. surpluses and deficits
For more than 50 years after the end of World War I in 1918 the United States managed to maintain a surplus on its balance of payments and was thus a creditor nation throughout this period. In the early 1970s, however, its position

began to be reversed, largely but not entirely because of the oil crisis that followed the Arab-Israeli Yom Kippur War in 1973. Over the next decade the United States ran a large current account deficit each year, and its overall financial position deteriorated so badly that it became a debtor nation. By the start of the 1990s the United States owed more money than any other nation in the world.

Throughout the 1980s and '90s the United States spent more on foreign goods and services than it earned through the sales of its goods and services to the rest of the world. U.S. firms learned the hard way that a balance-of-payments deficit is both a cause and an effect of low aggregate demand for a country's goods—foreigners buy less of a country's goods than before, and hence those goods tend to be less widely available in export markets. Goods that are not known to be available are less in demand than those that are on sale everywhere. It is a vicious circle.

The U.S. government could not allow this situation to continue and redressed the balance-of-payments deficit by reducing domestic consumption through cuts in welfare and numerous other government-funded services.

Visible and invisible trade

By contrast with the United States, the United Kingdom has traditionally imported more goods than it has sold abroad. Thus it has a deficit on what is known as visible trade. However, from the middle of the 19th century until the 1930s the nation more than compensated for this by invisible trade such as financial services, exchange controls, and the income derived from ownership of foreign and overseas banks.

In the 1940s, however, the United Kingdom was forced to liquidate most of its foreign assets to finance its involvement in World War II. After that it granted independence to nearly all the countries of its great overseas empire, which had once included Australia, Canada, Ghana, India, Kenya, New Zealand,

and Nigeria. The U.K. balance of payments then fell slowly but surely into deficit until in 1968 the government was forced to take steps to arrest the decline and make British goods more competitive in the international marketplace. It achieved this by devaluing its currency, the pound sterling.

Devaluation

A country that persistently runs a deficit in its balance of payments may ultimately be forced to devalue its currency because of the gradual depletion of its foreign exchange reserves. Devaluation reduces the exchange rate; and as a result imports become more expensive, and the country tends to import fewer goods. Domestically produced goods, however, become relatively cheaper on world markets, and the devaluing country will tend to export more of them. Thus the hoped for result of any devaluation is an increase in net exports that closes the current account deficit.

For the United Kingdom in 1968 devaluation was a way to pull out of the downward spiral of a balance-of-payments deficit. Devaluation may be useful in other circumstances, too. For example, during periods of high inflation a reduction in the value of the domestic currency against the currencies of other nations will make exports cheaper and, it is hoped, encourage foreigners to buy more goods from the devaluing nation.

The European Exchange Rate Mechanism (ERM), first set up in 1979, was designed to facilitate trade among European Union (EU) members by keeping their currencies within a predetermined band of value in relation to each other. The problem was that the weaker currencies found it difficult to make themselves as attractive to foreign investors as the stronger currencies, above all the German Deutsche mark. The Italian lira, one of the original members of the ERM, was forced to leave the system in 1992. It rejoined in 1996, but not before it had been devalued by 15 percent in order to attract foreign buyers.

ABOVE: One of the first dollar bills to be printed after U.S. Congress authorized the issue of paper money in March 1862.

The world's most traded currency

The U.S. dollar is the world's most actively traded currency, and because of this it serves monetary functions far beyond the boundaries of the United States. The dollar has become an intervention and reserve currency, a medium of exchange, a unit of account, and a store of value. The central banks of other countries hold large portions of their official international reserves in the form of U.S. dollars. Between 1990 and 1996 foreign central banks held an average of 55 percent of their official reserves in dollar denominated assets. Apart from the dollar, the world's other strongest currencies are the German mark and the Japanese yen. But during the same period foreign central banks held on average only 15 percent of their reserves in marks or mark-denominated assets and 8 percent of their reserves in yen or yen-denominated assets—these figures are eloquent testimony to the strength of the dollar.

The dollar's role as an international medium of exchange can be seen through its service as an international "third currency." If, for example, a Mexican bank needs Spanish pesetas, instead of buying the pesetas directly with its own Mexican pesos, the bank could well buy dollars for pesos and then use the dollars to buy pesetas. It is because of transactions such as this that the U.S. dollar market has become the largest part of the foreign exchange market in foreign exchange centers, and New York has become one of the largest such centers in the world. Of the $1.2 trillion average daily trading volume on the world's foreign exchange markets, 83 percent of all transactions involved the dollar, and 32 per cent of them occurred in the United States. In comparison, only 37 percent of transactions involved the German mark and 24 percent the Japanese yen.

The importance of the dollar's role as a unit of account can be seen in the number of international commercial contracts that are denominated in dollars (more common in raw material and commodity markets). Payment is frequently made in dollars—European countries use dollars to pay for oil from the Middle East, and Japan's imports of raw materials from Southeast Asia are largely denominated in dollars. It is estimated that between 50 and 70 percent of the stock of U.S. currency is now held outside the United States, illustrat-

BELOW: U.S. Trade Representative Charlene Barshefsky speaking at the press briefing on the 1999 meeting of the World Trade Organization in Seattle, Washington.

ing how individuals and businesses abroad have become accustomed to using the dollar as a store of value. In economically or politically unstable countries the use of the dollar as a store of value is particularly pronounced, and in Liberia and Panama the dollar is even used as the domestic currency.

Multilateralism versus regionalism

Since the end of World War II in 1945 many nations have pursued the objective of trade liberalization. Among the devices used to achieve this end were the GATT and its successor, the WTO, which came into being on January 1, 1995 (*see* box on page 57).

While the GATT began with fewer than 30 countries, the WTO currently has more than 130 members. The GATT and WTO agreements are sometimes known as "multilateral" approaches to trade liberalization. This is because membership commits nations to reduce trade barriers simultaneously. WTO in particular has the power and legal status to resolve trade disputes through independent panels. Its decisions have the force of law—a member may query rulings with the WTO Appeals Tribunal, but it must be bound by its verdict. The failure of a WTO member to abide by the body's judgment would subject it to trade sanctions.

The 1999 Seattle WTO Conference

The WTO meeting convened in Seattle, Washington, in November 1999 made its main target the further relaxation of remaining trading restrictions.

WTO has identified agriculture and the service industries as the areas in which there is currently the greatest potential for economic improvement. The United States, in particular, has been looking for global elimination of agricultural export subsidies, a drastic reduction in domestic price supports, and a steep cut in trade barriers, especially tariffs that protect certain favored farming sectors. In services, which now account for almost a quarter of all international trade, the United States wants barriers to foreign competition lowered across all sectors, with as few exceptions as possible.

Trade barriers against manufactured goods should be lowered aggressively, with tariffs now below 5 percent reduced to zero and those still above that level reduced to 5 percent with a view to phasing them out altogether. All duties on information technology (IT) should be eliminated, and international commerce on the Internet kept duty-free. Advanced economies should keep their com-

mitments to phase out all textile and clothes quotas by 2005. WTO antidumping rules should be tightened to prevent them being abused for protectionist purposes. The United States also wants the WTO dispute-settlement mechanism to be strengtheend so that countries that refuse to abide by its rulings are forced to implement further liberalization, rather than merely suffer sanctions.

Although the voice of the United States is the strongest in the WTO, these objectives are not unopposed. The EU, for example, is committed to protecting its farmers through the Common Agricultural Policy and will resist any moves to dismantle existing barriers. U.S. workers and trade unions also have grave concerns that the removal of all tariffs will threaten their jobs. At the same time, many people in the developing world fear that the abolition of all tariffs will favor only the most advanced nations in the West, and that the economies of poor countries will be rendered even poorer.

ABOVE: Cargo containers on a wharf at Newport, Wales. This form of transportation has revolutionized international trade.

Regional free-trade agreements

Although most countries are involved with WTO and broadly sympathetic to its aims, many nations attempt to achieve trade liberalization through the formation of preferential trade arrangements, free-trade areas, customs unions, and common markets. Since many of these agreements involve countries that are geographically contiguous or close to each other, these methods are sometimes referred to as a "regional" approach.

Regional trade arrangements are widely regarded as positive steps in the direction of completely free trade. Indeed, Section 24 of the original GATT allows signatory countries to form free-trade agreements and customs unions despite the fact that preferential agreements are regarded as violations of the principle of nondiscrimination. When a free-trade area or customs union is formed between two or more WTO member countries, those countries agree in effect to lower their tariffs between each other to zero but to maintain their tariffs against other WTO countries. Thus the free-trade area imposes discriminatory policies. These agreements are tolerated within the WTO because they repre-

sent significant commitments to free trade, which is the fundamental goal of the WTO.

However, there is some concern among economists that regional trade agreements may make it more difficult to achieve the ultimate objective of global free trade. The fear is that although regional trade agreements will liberalize trade among their member countries, such arrangements may also increase incentives to raise protectionist trade barriers against countries outside the area. The logic of this is that the larger the regional trade area relative to the size of the world market, the larger that region's market power in trade will be. The greater the market power, the higher the region's optimal tariffs and export taxes. Thus the regional approach to trade liberalization could lead to the formation of large trade blocs that trade freely among members but choke off trade with the rest of the world. For this reason some economists have now reached the conclusion that the multilateral approach to trade liberalization, represented by the agreements reached in successive WTO rounds, is more likely to achieve global free trade than any regional or preferential approach.

ABOVE: Not everyone believes that GATT and the WTO are good ideas. All over the world many people fear that these trade agreements favor the developed world and make poor countries even poorer.

SEE ALSO:

• Volume 1, page 71: Money markets and interest rates

• Volume 2, page 80: How firms behave in the real world

• Volume 5, page 41: Free trade and protectionism

• Volume 6, page 38: The age of reason and early industrialization

The world economy

The modern world economy binds together all regions of the globe, from the very rich to the very poor. Although the United States stands alone as the most influential political and economic power, it shares with the other economic regions certain general trends that are likely to change the nature of the global economy.

At the beginning of the 21st century the world economy retained many of the characteristics that had emerged in the second half of the 20th century. The United States remained the single largest economy, with a gross domestic product (GDP) of $7.434 trillion, followed by Japan and Germany with $5.149 trillion and $2.365 trillion respectively. The advanced industrial economies dominated world trade—the countries of the European Union had a combined GDP of $8.469 trillion; Africa and some parts of southern Asia remained home to the world's poorest nations. Some developing countries were severely handicapped by debts of billions of dollars to industrialized nations, some of whom began to cancel some debts in the hope of encouraging economic growth.

The global economy grew steadily but unevenly. Although world GDP grew by 3 percent from 1989 to 1996, for example, that of the G7—the seven leading industrialized nations—grew by only 1.9 percent, while China's GDP grew by 12.3 percent. In the same period many of the countries of the former Soviet Union experienced a decrease in GDP. In Georgia and Armenia GDP fell by over 20 percent. The extremes of growth and contraction related to two significant events in the final decades of the 20th century: the end of the communist system that dominated the Soviet Union and Eastern Europe, and China's enthusiastic embracing of a more capitalistic form of economics. With the world's largest population and vast natural resources, China had the potential to become one of the most powerful economic powers in the world.

A global economy

The defining characteristics of the late 20th-century world economy were its truly global nature, its tendency toward standardization of

RIGHT: The demolition of the Berlin Wall in 1989 led to the reunification of Germany in the following year. Despite the problems this caused, the new state soon recovered to become an enormous influence on the world economy.

business operations and the minimization of government regulation, and its organization into international trading areas. Negative characteristics included an overall slowdown in economic growth, a susceptibility to currency or financial market crises, and a trend toward the establishment of protectionist measures intended to safeguard domestic industries against foreign competition.

Trade and financial markets tied together economies on different sides of the world. The spillover effect of the financial crisis that struck East Asia in 1997, for example, spread rapidly to Europe and the United States, where falling exports to Asian countries had a marked negative effect on the balance of payments; the same currency destabilization that affected Thailand and Indonesia, meanwhile, also threatened to undermine the Brazilian currency.

Globalization

The interdependence of national economies is the result of a number of factors, including particularly advances in transportation, communications technology, and financial deregulation, the relaxation of laws that restricted trade, and the international movement of finance. International interdependence is part of a phenomenon known as globalization, which refers to the process by which the world's economic and technological forces are becoming incorporated into a single market. Along with the process go other forms of globalization: people on different continents increasingly watch the same TV shows, drink the same soda, dance to the same music, or wear clothes from the same designer stores. Globalization is a social and cultural phenomenon as well as an economic one.

Both a cause and a consequence of globalization is the emergence of multinationals, firms that have production facilities or factories in numerous countries. At the end of the century some 200 multinational corporations produced one-third of the world's total output. The output of some multinationals was larger than the GDP of even industrialized countries. The 100 largest multinationals employed six million workers worldwide.

Multinationals in some ways transcend the borders of nation-states. Firms such as Pepsi, Mitsubishi, McDonalds, IBM, Ford, or Nestlé can locate their operations among countries in search of less economic regulation, cheaper labor, or cheaper raw materials.

Many economists welcome globalization and the operations of multinationals as subjecting all business to the discipline of the marketplace. On a more practical level supporters of globalization argue that investment by a multinational greatly benefits a national

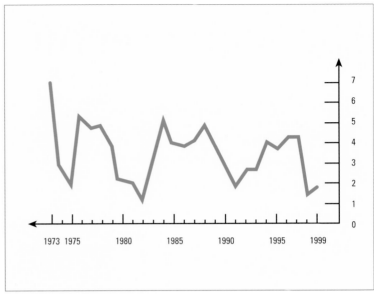

Figure 1 Change in world GDP (%)

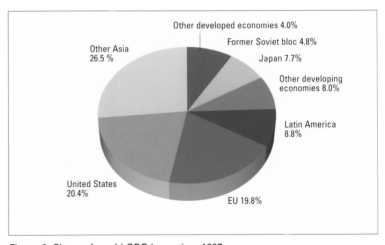

Figure 2 Share of world GDP by region, 1997

economy, particularly in a developing country, by stimulating trade and general rises in the standard of living.

At the end of the 20th century the Organization for Economic Cooperation and Development (OECD) studied the impact of multinationals on domestic economies where they had affiliates. It discovered that the share of manufacturing output produced by foreign firms is growing in many economies. In the United States in 1996, for example, foreign firms produced 15.8 percent of manufacturing output, up from 8.8 percent a little over a decade earlier in 1985. In Ireland multinationals produced 66 percent of output and employed more than half of all workers.

Critics of multinationals point out that, particularly in the undeveloped or developing world, they have the power to drive local producers out of a market, reducing competition and consumer choice, and removing

ABOVE: The world GDP followed a downward trend in the last quarter of the 20th century.

profits from the country's economy. Large multinationals have been accused of keeping wages low and of being less concerned with health and safety regulation in developing countries than in the industrialized world.

The OECD suggested differently, however. It found that on average, foreign firms paid their local workers more than domestic firms did. In the United States they paid 6 percent more in 1996 than American firms. In a poorer country, such as Turkey, the difference is even more pronounced. Workers in multinational firms earn 124 percent above average wages for the country. The OECD also identified other benefits of multinational investment in an economy. Foreign firms were creating jobs quicker than domestic ones; they were spending more on research and development than domestic firms; and they tended to export more of their output than domestic producers. In Turkey, for example, the multinational workforce has risen 11.5 percent a year, compared with a 0.6 percent rise in the domestic workforce, and multinationals spent twice as much on research and development as Turkish firms.

Deregulation

The world economy at the end of the 20th century was characterized by the global dominance of free-market capitalism. For much of the century communism had inspired experiments in planned economies, with state control of production and distribution. The most significant of these experiments were in the Soviet Union (from 1917) and China (from 1949), but smaller nations such as Vietnam, Cuba, and Ethiopia also established economies that were regulated by central government to a greater or lesser degree. Planned economies were characterized by the predominance of heavy industry and weak consumer production. Eventually, they proved a failure. The collapse of communism in Eastern Europe in 1989 and the breakup of the Soviet Union were at least partly the result of the inability of the Eastern bloc's economy to keep up with the military spending of the United States. For those who saw the Cold War as a conflict between capitalist democracy on one side and authoritarian communism on the other, capitalism had triumphed.

One of the consequences was the removal of a considerable amount of regulation on business. Firms now faced similar laws in virtually all countries and shared the same goal: making a profit in the open marketplace. Whereas a factory in the Soviet Union and one in the United States had once been subject to very different legislation, they now were both increasingly subject to only one regulation, that of the market and the forces that drove it.

Trading blocs emerged as neighboring countries grouped together to remove barriers to trade such as tariffs. The North American

ABOVE: The East Asian economic boom led to grand building projects, such as this opulent shopping mall in Kuala Lumpur, Malaysia.

Bust, boom, and bust

If the East Asian crash began on July 2, 1997, with the floating of the Thai *baht*, the boom that triggered it was itself begun nearly ten years earlier on October 19, 1987, the notorious "Black Monday." That was the day the Dow Jones stock index lost 22.6 percent of its value, and U.S. investors looked to fresh fields. The tiger economies—the booming nations of the Pacific Rim—were an obvious target.

Over the next decade $500 billion flowed into Southeast Asia from abroad, mainly from the United States and Europe. Much of this money was invested in untried companies by young, inexperienced financial managers. In 1996, on the crest of the wave, Southeast Asia seemed to possess all the most positive economic indicators, from phenomenal growth to the world's newly opened largest building. A year later it had all evaporated, and the tigers were left to lick their wounds.

Tourism: the world's largest industry

Although the world economy may seem to be dominated by automobile manufacture and agricultural produce, which have highly visible outputs, the largest industry is in fact travel and tourism combined. Even before they achieved their current preeminence, travel and tourism had been established for years as the world's largest nonagricultural employer, with one in every 15 workers around the world occupied to some extent in organizing, transporting, housing, feeding, guiding, or entertaining tourists.

According to statistics compiled by the World Travel and Tourism Council, in 1996 the travel and tourist industry:
- generated an output of $3.6 trillion
- contributed 10.7 percent of global gross domestic product
- employed 225 million people
- invested $766 billion in capital projects
- generated $761 billion in world exports
- paid $653 billion in taxes worldwide

The receipts of the tourist industry increased by a factor of 20 in a quarter of a century—from $17.9 billion in 1970 to $371.7 billion in 1995. There were several reasons for this enormous growth. Among the most important were increased wealth and leisure time, the advent of cheap air travel, and a general increase in people's lifestyle expectations and a broadening of their horizons.

Who travels and where?
Nearly 593 million people traveled abroad in 1996, an increase of 4.6 percent on 1995. In terms of the total number of visitors received, the United States (7.89 percent of the world total) ranked well behind France (10.68 percent) and Spain (7.96 percent), but received a great deal more income from their tourists: over $64 billion in 1996 (over 15 percent of the global total), compared with France and Spain (both $28 billion) and Italy ($27 billion).

ABOVE: The Pyramids of Egypt—which were among the Seven Wonders of the Ancient World—have lost some of their appeal through pollution and too many people flocking to see them. Nevertheless, the Egyptian economy would struggle without tourism.

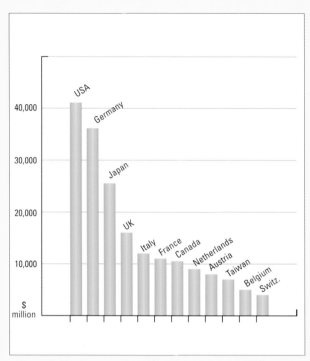

Figure 3 Tourist spending: who spent the most, 1996.

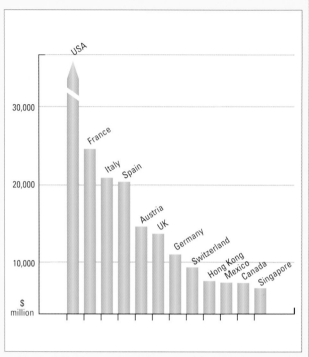

Figure 4 Tourist earning: who earned the most in 1996.

Most of the world's governments encourage tourists to visit their countries purely on economic grounds: tourism generates employment—even though much of the work is often only seasonal—and brings in substantial foreign revenues. Some countries—indeed, entire regions such as the islands of the Caribbean and many Mediterranean coastal areas—are heavily or even totally reliant on tourism. However, the organizing companies and the airlines often gain even more from a package vacation than the country visited. The destination region typically pulls in only around 40 percent of the total revenue. If the package deal involves a foreign-owned hotel, the host country may receive an even smaller percentage of the total amount generated, sometimes raking in as little as 20 percent of the total cost of the package.

Tourism—the downside
While international tourism is enormously profitable, it may, if not carefully nurtured, contain the seeds of its own destruction. Beautiful places may lose their appeal once everyone starts to visit them at roughly the same times of year. This is already a problem in such popular destinations as Yosemite Valley in California, the Grand Canyon in Arizona, and, further afield, Australia's Great Barrier Reef. Local cultures may be corrupted as short-sighted governments and get-rich-quick property developers build ever more airports, roads, hotels, casinos, theme parks, and other leisure facilities. Unless these developments are carefully planned and sensitively executed, they may become eyesores that destroy the appeal that brought the influx of visitors in the first place.

As American environmental expert Joni Seager has put it: "Tourism has become a quasi-industrial process, in which the landscape, habitat, wildlife, and local people all become consumable goods. High-volume tourism overwhelms local facilities for water supply, sewage treatment, and municipal waste disposal."

While large-scale resort-based tourism seems reluctant to heed these warnings, some environment-based concerns have developed the practice of what is known as "sustainable tourism." Visitors' activities are regulated to ensure that they cause minimal environmental damage—they are taken walking by guides, for example, who steer them away from fragile areas— and the revenue they produce is used for the careful management of the area. The national parks of Cameroon and Costa Rica (which comprise a quarter of its territory) are prime examples. This "green" or "ecotourism" emphasizes environmental protection while minimizing damaging tourist activities.

Many modern tourist ecopackages, however, remain little more than standard vacations with a "green" varnish. Unless radical changes occur in the expectations of the tourists themselves, as well as those who profit from them, most of the world's premier destinations could be overrun or irreparably spoiled by the early part of this century.

As the 21st century dawns, traditional tourist resorts face an uncertain future. If they continue to be inundated, they will lose their inherent attraction. And if there is a severe recession in the advanced nations—more than 70 percent of the world's tourists come from the 10 wealthiest nations—the world's most lucrative destinations could simply become economic white elephants.

Free Trade Agreement included the United States, Mexico, and Canada; the European Community brought most of Europe into a free-trade zone (*see* page 86).

Economic slowdown

In 1999 the International Monetary Fund predicted a global economic slowdown, although it also saw positive developments such as the growth of the U.S. economy and the low levels of inflation in many developed economies. The slowdown itself was partly a consequence of the globalization of the world economy. Since 1997 the deregulation of financial markets, which facilitates international currency dealing, had exacerbated recurrent bouts of instability in global financial markets. Economic or political upheavals in one economy could affect others, a phenomenon known as contagion, making the stability of emerging market economies such as China, where the financial sector remains fragile, important to all economies. The crisis that struck Thailand and then much of East Asia in 1997 resulted in the contraction of not just the regional but the global economy.

The western economies survived the effects of the Asian crash of 1997 relatively well, as they did a similar crisis in Brazil, the world's eighth-largest economy, the following year. Economists point out, however, that in a global economy there are always numerous potential sources of further turbulence. Russia, which itself went through an economic crisis in the summer of 1998, remained politically unstable and economically immature. The numerous conflicts that broke out in the former Yugoslavia had an adverse effect on neighboring countries and thus on the economy of southern Europe. Japan, the world's second-largest economy, was in recession.

Many economists fear the potential consequences of contagion in financial markets. They advocate the use of fiscal and monetary policy to limit its effects and also warn against overvalued exchange rates by which a currency is pegged to an unreasonably high value of a stronger currency. National governments, meanwhile, have been tempted to reestablish protectionist measures in an attempt to fend off contagion.

World trade

Like the world economy, world trade in the late 20th century was dominated by the United States. In 1996 the United States was responsible for 14.22 percent of the world's exports, including both visible exports such as raw materials or manufactured goods and invisible exports, which include services such as insurance and other financial services that

ABOVE: Hundreds of South Korean homeless line up to receive free food at a plaza in front of a railroad station in the capital, Seoul. Thousands lost their jobs and their homes in the economic crash of 1998.

account for about one-quarter of international trade. The United States exports largely capital goods, consumer goods, and industrial supplies to trading partners that include Canada, Japan, and Mexico.

World trade as a whole is characterized by the movement of natural resources, such as minerals, fuel, and agricultural produce, and that of manufactured goods. In the past trade was to some extent a circular process: developing countries often supplied raw materials to the industrialized world, which in return shipped back finished manufactured goods.. Globalization and the relocation of factories by multinationals eager to find sources of cheap labor and supplies, however, mean that many of the developing countries are now also major exporters of finished industrial and consumer goods.

World economic regions

The modern world economy can be divided into roughly six main zones. Some, like the European Union, are formal political or economic entities. Some, like the Indian subcontinent, also called South Asia, are largely geographical entities that might or might not share a political outlook but which are nevertheless bound in an identifiable trading unit. The most powerful economic zone is made up of the members of the North American Free Trade Agreement, the United States,

Canada, and Mexico (*see* page 105). Although the United States dominates the relationship, both Canada and Mexico are sizable economic powers, ranking respectively as the ninth and sixteenth largest economies in the world. Canada has a highly developed motor vehicle industry and rich supplies of timber, minerals, and agricultural produce; Mexico is a major exporter of oil and energy.

East Asia

Between 1990 and 1995 six of the 10 countries with the highest average growth in GDP were in East Asia: China (12 percent), Malaysia (8.7 percent), Thailand (8.6 percent), Singapore (8.5 percent), Vietnam (8.2 percent), and South Korea (7.5 percent). With strong government support and cheap labor these countries produced a range of products—notably cars and electronics equipment—at prices the West could not match. Despite rapid growth and rising living standards, however, the so-called "tiger" economies had financial weaknesses that were exposed by the crisis of 1997.

The crisis began on July 2, 1997, when the Thai government freed its currency, the baht, from being pegged to the U.S. dollar. By floating the baht, Thailand managed to avoid defaulting on its international debt payments, but the currency sank like a stone. The government was unable to prop it up. The country's reported reserves of more than $30 billion were a myth. The actual figure was $1.14 billion, comparable to only a couple of days' trade.

The collapse of the baht was followed by a chain reaction across Southeast Asia as investors pulled out of Malaysia, Indonesia, and South Korea. The value of most currencies in the region fell between 40 percent and 60 percent. The Indonesian rupiah plunged 80 percent by March 1998.

Toward the end of 1997 South Korea announced that it could not meet its external debt repayments. In five months 70,000 businesses had gone bankrupt, and unemployment had soared from 2.5 percent to 8.5 percent. Growth for 1998 was predicted to fall from 5.5 percent to virtually zero.

LEFT: At the heart of the world economy lies trade, most of which depends on the physical transfer of goods from one place to another: by road, rail, sea, or air.

The crisis was partly the result of the relatively primitive structure of Asian financial institutions, but there were many other contributory factors. Malaysia suffered labor shortages, for example, while in Indonesia the corrupt government of President Suharto took $30 billion out of the economy for itself. Among other factors, American, Japanese, and European companies and banks had invested heavily in the region, fueling a speculative boom without questioning the region's basic economic strength. Foreign investment averaged 37 percent of GDP in the region, reaching 43 percent in Malaysia. As early as 1994, in *Time* magazine, Massachusetts Institute of Technology economics professor Paul Krugman was pointing to the law of diminishing returns operating in Southeast Asia. The boom could not last, he predicted. When it ended in 1997, foreign investors rushed to convert their long-term assets into cash and their local currencies into U.S. dollars.

Not all nations in the region caught the "Asian flu." China moved into the export markets left by the crisis-struck nations. Hong Kong saw no serious withdrawal of investment. Taiwan and Singapore, older and more stable economies, escaped largely unscathed.

BELOW: The East Asian economies slowed down dramatically in 1997, and GDP suffered negative growth in 1998.

ABOVE: The Chinese flag is raised in Hong Kong on July 1, 1997, in a ceremony marking the end of British colonial rule.

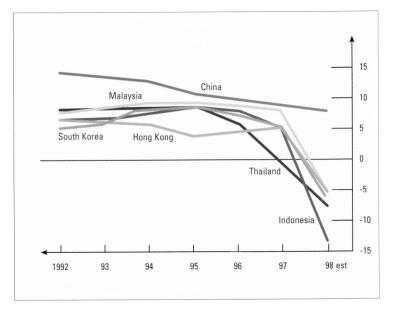

Figure 5 Annual change in GDP of East Asian economies (%)

Hong Kong—Crown jewel

On July 1, 1997, the crown colony of Hong Kong was passed by the British back into the hands of the Chinese government that had leased it to them 155 years earlier. While China added only six million people to its population of almost 1.3 billion, it also inherited a crucially important economic power base.

The statistics are remarkable. Beijing now owned the world's largest container port, the world's greatest exporter of clothes, and the world's tenth-biggest trader.

It has yet to be seen how well the free-market economy of Hong Kong will coexist with the mainland's rigid political control. The Chinese themselves intend to combine their communist politics with capitalist economics. Although the sheltered waters between Victoria and Kowloon offer one of the world's finest natural harbors, the fortunes of this dynamic, densely populated community have been founded on manufacturing, banking, and commerce. The territory's greatest resources have been the ingenuity and acumen of its people, and only time will tell if these capitalistic attributes will continue to flourish inside the world's largest communist state.

It is perhaps ironic that the Asian crash of 1997 began in Bangkok the very day after the changeover in Hong Kong. If it was an early examination of the new arrangement, the territory passed with distinction. While there was panic selling on the Hong Kong stock exchange—a rival to Tokyo and Frankfurt for third spot behind London and New York—there was reassuringly little flight of crucial capital.

The Hong Kong of the future could prove an effective compromise: all the benefits of the free market but within the constraints of a controlling socialist regime not forced to face the consequences of free-market cycles of boom and bust. Conversely, it could prove to be a fudged failure, with the faults of both systems and the benefits of neither. Economists watch Hong Kong's development with great interest.

ABOVE: Although China is a communist state, it has a complex relationship with capitalism. Its financial center is the port of Shanghai, where new offices and factories are springing up all the time.

BELOW: Although GDP reflects the value of the output of an economy, it does not relate it to prices in the economy. Applying present purchasing power (PPP) exchange rates produces a new ranking that takes into account how much the GDP is really worth.

institutions to make a quick return to reinvest. South Korea initially rejected outside assistance before the International Monetary Fund (IMF) arranged an $8 billion rescue package, a figure dwarfed by the $45 billion fund that it arranged for crippled Indonesia. Meanwhile there was a collapse of demand within the region itself that further reduced production. In 1998 GDP fell by 6 percent in Malaysia, 8 percent in Thailand, and 14 percent in Indonesia. Two years after the crash, however, there were already signs that recovery was occuring. Exports rose, interest rates fell, liquidity returned to capital markets, and foreign investors reappeared, most significantly from the European Union. South Korea was the first country to show signs of a return to normal, with 2 or 3 percent growth forecast for 1999.

Panic spread far beyond Asia, however. Nations as diverse as Ukraine, Egypt, and South Africa were in danger of falling victim to the disease. In some cases only prompt action by the U.S. Treasury to prop up national economies helped avert crisis.

Bringing the tigers to heel

Following the crash politicians were quick to point the finger of blame at others. Malaysia's Prime Minister Mahathir Mahomad cited a host of foreign individuals and organizations as the culprits. Such claims hardly inspired

Calculations Change the Relative Size of Nations 1994		
Country	GDP using market exchange rates ($ billions)	GDP using PPP exchange rates ($ billions)
United States	6,648	6,648
Japan	4,591	2,802
Germany	2,046	1,558
India	294	1,174
France	1,330	1,117
United Kingdom	1,017	997
Indonesia	175	714
Russia	377	655
Mexico	377	635
Philippines	64	184
Malaysia	71	171
Nigeria	35	150
Hong Kong	132	128

Japan: sunrise to sunset

The extent and speed of East Asia's recovery probably depend on Japan, by far the largest economy in the region and the second-largest in the world. Many western experts, however, see Japan itself as a cause of the East Asian crisis rather than its solution.

After the U.S. postwar occupation ended in 1952, Japan recovered quickly through the efficient use of technology and grew so rapidly through the early 1990s that the economy might have become larger than that of the United States by the end of the century. The boom was based on excessive borrowing, however, and in the late 1990s an economic crisis hit. The stock market fell by more than 50 percent, and despite government efforts, many businesses collapsed, including the country's oldest investment bank, Yamaichi.

In 1998 a 3 percent contraction in the economy forced Japan into a trillion-dollar New Deal-style package of rescue measures designed to stimulate growth. It was a radical move for a nation that traditionally tried to save rather than spend to avoid recession, but many economists believed that Japan needed a radical root-and-branch reform of the entire financial system. Most experts predicted around zero growth for Japan in 1999, despite the country having the largest peacetime budget deficit ever recorded, and a return to real growth in 2000 or perhaps 2001.

As a British news correspondent described Japan's recession in August 1999: "The second richest country in the world is sleepwalking into the twenty-first century. In the past it grew its way out of any problems. Those days are over now."

China: the sleeping giant awakes

China, the world's most populous state, remains largely agricultural and ruled by a communist government. Since the death of Communist Party Chairman Mao Zedong in 1976, however, China's economic planners have stressed the need for economic modernization along western, capitalist lines. Rich in coal, iron, oil, and other resources, China suffered from a lack of financial capital and technology. As in other former communist states, the Chinese leadership loosened many economic restrictions. They set up special economic zones (SEZs) to promote development, encouraged well-policed foreign investment, and exploited the advantages of their "most-favored-nation" status with the United States. Unlike in other countries, however, China's economic modernization did not bring political change. The country remains a one-party state—capitalism and democracy are not always inevitable partners—but some economists argue that the bureaucracy and corruption of the communist system limit China's potential for growth.

Despite reservations about China's political intentions and its poor record on human rights, U.S. and European governments have courted its rulers in the hope of gaining access to its domestic market of 1.3 billion people. China itself, having discouraged the kind of speculative inward investment that had stimulated growth in the other economies of East Asia but also weakened them, had little "hot money" to be pulled out.

China used the Asian crisis to increase its share in export markets. Like the other Asian economies, however, China cannot rely solely on exports. It can only achieve economic expansion through internal growth.

South Asia

If East Asia faced problems of returning to economic growth, neighboring South Asia—which includes India, Pakistan, Bangladesh, and Nepal—faced continuing problems caused at least in part by explosive population growth. It is home to 1.5 billion people and three of the world's ten most populous

BELOW: The President of Japan's Yamaichi Bank breaks down as he admits responsibility for the bank's collapse in 1998.

nations. India, with the second-highest population in the world after China, has a smaller economy than the Netherlands or Australia. South Asia is home to around four in ten of the world's poor. In tiny Nepal, which is in the bottom 20 countries of per capita GDP in the world, the average citizen generates just $200 every year.

At 5.2 percent the region's GDP growth in 1997 was down by nearly 1 percent from 1996, due mainly to sluggish demand in parts of India's industrial sector and low cotton output in Pakistan. In 1998, however, all four major countries registered growth rates between 5 percent and 6 percent. Despite such growth and an increase in foreign investment in the region, it remains an investment backwater. Only 3.6 percent of net private long-term investment flows to the developing countries goes to South Asia. It remains on the economic fringe, accounting for only about 1 percent of world trade.

Exploding populations

There are a number of reasons for South Asia's relatively weak economic position. They include a relatively underdeveloped industrial base, relatively low standards of literacy, and substantial international debt. Of fundamental importance, however, is the hostile relationship between India and Pakistan, the two major powers in the region.

India, a largely Hindu country, and Muslim Pakistan have since their creation in 1948 disputed control of the province of Kashmir. In the second half of the 1990s a number of high-profile incidents—not least the shooting down by India of a Pakistan navy aircraft in August 1999—continually threatened peace in the region. Uncertainty increased in May 1998 when both countries detonated nuclear devices, leading to the imposition of economic sanctions by several industrial nations led by the United States and Britain. In 1999 the prime minister of Pakistan was overthrown by a military coup, largely as a result of widespread dissatisfaction with economic progress, while Pakistan became more closely affiliated with the fundamentalist Islamic Taliban that controlled most of neighboring Afghanistan.

Positive signs

Positive economic signs for the region came in a significant rise in exports, even though the ratio of the value of exports to the amount of international debt the region owes is still lower than the average for developing nations. South Asia also managed to avoid painful spillover from the East Asian crisis thanks to its low levels of short-term external debt, small current account deficits, and financial regulation. India, in particular, attracted

increasing amounts of foreign investment in the last decade of the 20th century. In addition to its vast natural resources, the country is now developing thriving high-tech industries and an extensive service sector that benefits from a high population that keeps labor costs low.

ABOVE: Rice winnowing in Katmandu, the capital of Nepal. Nepal is one of the South Asian countries that has maintained steady if unspectacular growth through much of the 1990s.

North Africa and the Middle East

The economy of the Middle East is dominated by oil. Of the 14 countries in the world that derive more than 75 percent of their export revenue from crude oil, 10 are located in the Middle East and North Africa. Their closely tied interests are powerfully represented by OPEC, the Organization of Petroleum Exporting Countries. The Middle East alone accounts for more than 10 percent of the world's entire energy production. The region is also home to a handful of states that are not blessed with "black gold," however, and countries like Yemen, Palestine, Jordan, and Lebanon face the problems common to the developing world of debt and poverty.

Politically, the region is dominated by the tensions caused by the rise of Islamic funda-

The peace dividend: a false dream

The dramatic collapse of the Soviet empire, the democratization of Eastern Europe, and the end of the Cold War raised huge hopes for reductions in military spending and the diversion of those colossal funds into more peaceful channels. New initiatives would help to heal the wounds that the ideological divide between capitalism and communism had created 70 years previously. Humanitarians and environmentalists looked forward to monies formerly spent on armaments being made available to develop Third World that had until now been pawns in the struggle for influence between the superpowers.

While a few pockets of potential confrontation remained—the division of Korea and the geopolitical position of Cuba were the most obvious anomalies—by 1990 the Cold War was almost at an end. At last, went the argument, America and Russia could cut their armies and their armories. The MAD phase (mutually assured destruction) was effectively over.

Coming only 14 months after the fall of the Berlin Wall, the Gulf War severely delayed such measures. The western powers, and the United States in particular, realized that there would always be a need for military preparedness. If the old threat of international Marxism was now dead, there would always be loose-cannon dictators, fanatical Muslim fundamentalists, resurgent Russian communists, Latin American revolutionaries, and countries as unstable as India and Pakistan experimenting with nuclear tests. The point was driven home at the end of the decade with the potentially dangerous problems of Kosovo.

Deflating defense

Defense spending has indeed fallen. In the United States it almost halved as a proportion of GDP between 1986 and 1998, from 6.2 percent of GDP to 3.2 percent, the lowest level since World War II and equivalent to around $100 billion a year in 1997. The immediate effect was the loss of over a million jobs, with related employment falling by perhaps three times that amount. For many companies and their workers, therefore, international stability was hardly a benefit.

But there is a far broader economic picture. The demobilization of the Cold War economy has been on a smaller scale than the downscaling that took place after the two world wars, but it nevertheless followed the same course, initially blunting demand before the period of adjustment gave way to increased trade as a result of reduced international tensions.

Since the end of the Cold War, world trade has indeed mushroomed—by over 70 percent from 1989 to 1997, according to the International Monetary Fund (IMF). Yet virtually none of this has been directly attributable to the removal of the Iron Curtain: trade between the U.S. and the former Soviet bloc is still almost negligible. Meanwhile, the average defense spending of the world's nations is about 6 percent of GDP, with some countries—oil-rich Arab states, for example—shelling out up to 20 percent.

Jonathon Porritt, U.K. director of Friends of the Earth, wrote in 1990: "Even a straightforward reduction in arms spending, with no subsequent reallocation of the funds saved to promote sustainable development in the Third World, would bring enormous

ABOVE: *A display of warheads at the 1997 IDEF International Arms Fair in Ankara, Turkey.*

benefits, simply in terms of the metric tons of steel, barrels of oil, megawatts of energy, and depletion of precious metals that will no longer be poured down the global drain in the futile pursuit of military superiority."

In the United States, for example, it was hoped that lower defense spending would give federal and state governments an opportunity to spend more on education, health, and housing. Yet here, as in western Europe and the Soviet bloc, there has been no widespread transfer of resources to social programs.

Instead, the monies were a significant factor in the reduction of budget deficits. Between 1989 and 1998 the U.S. federal deficit fell from $220 billion to $50 billion, and in 1999 President Bill Clinton claimed credit for eliminating it altogether.

The fiscal benefit has led to a drop in interest rates and a continued expansion of the U.S. economy. The private sector, flush with funds, has burgeoned and taken up much of the slack caused by the fallout from reduced spending on defense.

Détente dividends

The transfer of resources to other sectors of the economy is one of the big dividends of détente. Large-scale military projects are costly and inefficient. Britain's Trident missile program proved to be a white elephant, and the French nuclear strategy was unnec-

essarily expensive. Nondefense investment is in the long term more productive.

Meanwhile, few nations divert their newly available funds to the Third World. Unless there is an economic or political strategy—as for example when U.S. companies raced to invest in post-Apartheid South Africa—the underdeveloped countries are regarded as not worth exploiting. Just as Russia pulled the plug on aid to Cuba, the United States no longer feels compelled to bolster faltering regimes in Africa, Asia, or Latin America. There has been no proportionate increase in aid from the international organizations funded by the leading capitalist powers.

The Third World can wait. After the end of the Cold War, it seemed as if victorious westerners with no vision of the real future of the world were too busy getting rich.

In their hopes for a global dividend, environmentalists such as Jonathon Porritt may have underestimated the basic acquisitive drives of capitalism, whether the beneficiaries are governments, company directors, shareholders, or individual workers glad of employment. "The thousands of millions of dollars a year that would become available," Porritt wrote, "could and should be used as the means of converting dreams into reality." It seems that such a prediction may prove overoptimistic.

ABOVE: *A child digging in Ethiopia, one of the Third World countries to have suffered most from the developed nations' indifference to their development and welfare.*

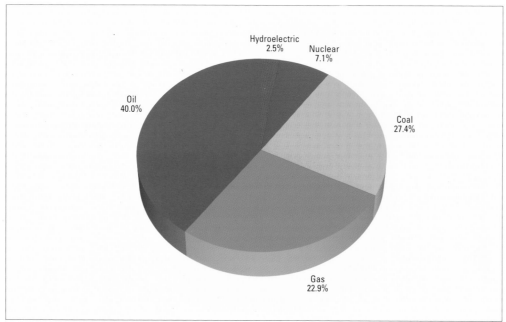

Figure 6 World sources of energy, 1997.

LEFT: Oil remains the world's major source of energy, suggesting that the Middle East will retain its wealth and economic power.

mentalism in countries such as Algeria, where Muslims reject what they see as decadent western and capitalist values, and the existence of the Jewish state of Israel among the nations of the Arab world. Israel has no oil, few other natural resources, and little water. Per capita, Israelis are the world's greatest recipients of economic aid, mainly from the United States. Over 30 percent of Israel's exports—mostly in the shape of metals, diamonds, and chemicals—go to the United States to repay some of the debt.

Winners and losers

In 1997 most countries in the region achieved growth rates of between 4 and 6 percent, an improvement on the previous decade, when growth had been restricted by falling oil prices. The dependence on oil and the lack of a large industrial base or consumer sector left many parts of the region vulnerable to external influences, however. Drought in Morocco and Algeria limited growth to virtually zero, while the slow progress of the Middle East peace process disrupted growth in Palestine and Israel's other neighbors.

The region also suffers from sharp disparities in income and status. The United Arab Emirates, for example, boasts the highest per capita GDP in Asia after Japan and Singapore, but only one-fifth of its population are citizens of the state. The other four-fifths are disenfranchised immigrant workers from less wealthy Middle East countries and poor Islamic nations, predominantly Pakistan. Immigrant workers perform many of the more menial tasks. The other wealthy Gulf states have a similar demographic profile.

The way forward?

Some economists wonder whether the semifeudal structure and centralized economies of many oil-rich countries, which are ruled by unelected monarchs or military dictators, can achieve socioeconomic progress and economic expansion. They believe that the private sector should be developed in order to drive economic growth.

The government of Saudi Arabia, the area's richest nation, planned to introduce privatization to reduce the burden on the all-providing state but claimed that privatizing electricity alone would cost around $120 billion. Critics argue that privatization could easily be financed by recalling the $500 billion that privileged Saudis have invested abroad.

Although western observers condemn the Middle East's lack of political representation and freedom of choice, citizens in many Middle Eastern nations enjoy some benefits. They do not have to pay taxes—public expenditure is funded by oil revenues—and contribute nothing for their extensive healthcare, education, and social welfare services. Ordinary people enjoy a standard of living unimaginable before the oil boom. For the nations of North Africa, where earnings are supported by tourism and, in the case of Algeria, by abundant supplies of natural gas, the short- to midterm picture is also optimistic.

Sub-Saharan Africa

While the developing countries of the world enjoy some of the fastest rates of growth in GDP, the underdeveloped or undeveloped nations do not always share in the general

Case study: The 1970s oil crisis

The greatest threat to the world economy in the second half of the 20th century was the oil crisis, which began after the Yom Kippur War between the Arabs and Israel in October 1973.

At their 35th conference at Vienna, Austria, in the fall of 1973, the 11 members of OPEC raised the price of crude petroleum by 70 percent. Then in December, at Tehran, Iran, they voted a staggering hike of nearly 130 percent, adding an embargo on shipments to the United States. The Tehran decisions were political, generated by the dominant Middle East nations of OPEC in retaliation for U.S. support of Israel during the Yom Kippur War. Despite some internal opposition, notably from Saudi Arabia, subsequent increases took the price of oil from less than $3 a barrel in 1973 to a peak of $34 in 1981.

For the advanced nations the rises were almost catastrophic. Governments and firms were forced into part-time operations as alternative sources of oil were found, with Mexico and the Soviet Union being particular beneficiaries. However, coming in the wake of the 1971 collapse of the Bretton Woods system for fixing currency exchange rates (*see* page 94), and in the middle of a period of "stagflation," the increases triggered a major reversal of the postwar industrial boom in the United States.

The economic prosperity of the 1950s had continued into the 1960s, during which GNP had risen by 50 percent, and the average American family enjoyed a real increase of more than 30 percent in its disposable income. In contrast, by 1979 the typical family had only 7 percent more real purchasing power than it had had in 1969.

The 1970s saw increases in unemployment and inflation; and in 1971, for the first time in the 20th century, the United States recorded a negative trade balance. This loss was repeated in 19 of the following 21 years. For Americans, already reeling from their expensive failure in Vietnam, the realization that everyday life could be so affected by a few wealthy Arabs thousands of miles away came as a real shock to the national psyche.

However, the United States was not suffering alone. In many ways Western Europe and Japan, lacking any significant reserves of oil, fared even worse. Between 1973 and 1978 rates of growth in the OECD countries plunged to around 2.5 percent.

In Europe, Belgium, Sweden, and especially France accelerated the development of their nuclear power programs, while Britain and Norway hurried to extract oil from below the floor of the North Sea. Multinationals began to explore and produce oil in areas that were previously thought too difficult or uneconomical, including Alaska and demanding offshore sites. More thought was now given to conservation and alternative sources of energy.

By 1982 the West's reduced dependence on OPEC oil had forced the cartel to reduce both production and prices. OPEC's unity was weakened during the 1980s, principally by the Iran-Iraq War, in which Saudi Arabia—owner of the greatest oil reserves—was commonly a dissenting voice. In 1986 the Saudis drove down oil prices in spectacular fashion, cutting the cost of crude from $28 to $10 a barrel. Although this reduction was not as great as the 1973 rise, it signified that the oil crisis had run its course.

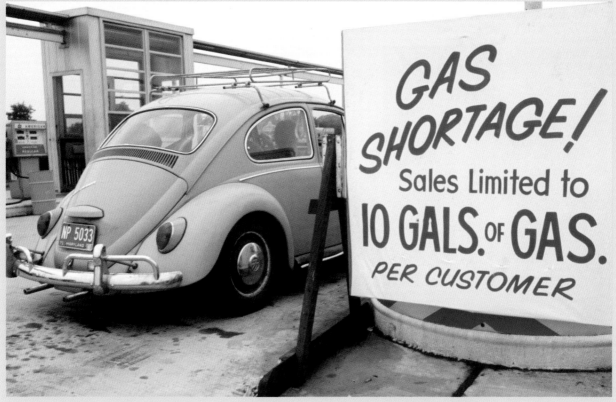

ABOVE: *The post-1973 oil crisis led to gas rationing in the United States.*

economic growth. Many such nations lie in the southern part of Africa, south of the vast Sahara Desert, home to 15 of the 20 countries with the lowest GDP per capita in 1996. There are only two sub-Saharan nations, Nigeria and South Africa, that have more than one-quarter of one percent of world trade. Starved of genuine investment, dozens of African states seem locked into a cycle of poverty and debt.

At the heart of the problems of the poor African nations lies a selection of interrelated, seemingly intractable problems. Foremost is overpopulation: many countries find it difficult to produce enough food to support their citizens, a problem that is worsening as populations rise. In 1994 Africa produced 27 percent less food per head than in 1967. The problem is made worse by periodic floods and droughts, environmental degradation, and civil wars. Malnutrition leads to disease, illiteracy levels are high, and poor transportation and communications limit the development of markets on anything larger than a local scale. Despotism and corruption often handicap political development. In the 1990s AIDs became a serious problem, especially in East Africa: The World Health Organization (WHO) estimates that the region accounts for over 70 percent of the world's cases.

There are some encouraging statistics. In 1997, for example, there was average sub-Saharan growth for the third year in succession, with 21 nations reporting increases of 5 percent or more. But such developments come from such a low starting point that they

LEFT: A mother and child on the road in the Sahel, the semiarid African region that extends from Senegal east to Sudan.

LEFT: A geologist examines a sample in a gold mine in South Africa. Africa's vast mineral wealth is one of the most important sectors of its economy, along with agriculture.

are misleading. They cannot be compared with similar percentage rises in America, Europe, East Asia, or Australasia.

Neocolonialism

In some countries the economic power of industrialized markets and western firms dictates economic priorities to the detriment of the local economy, a relationship known as neocolonialism that is often reinforced by the debts Africa owes to developed countries. Nations such as Angola, Nigeria, and Zaire, which are rich in natural resources, tend to remain overdependent on a single resource for export or on one or two cash crops. Their economies remain highly vulnerable to instability caused by a crop failure or a fall in world commodity prices.

Wide-ranging examples include minerals—oil from Gabon and Nigeria, where it represents 95 percent of export earnings, or copper from Zaire and Zambia (more than 90 percent)—and more specialized commodities such as titanium ore or rutile from Sierra Leone, phosphates from Togo, uranium from Namibia, and diamonds from Botswana. The same overreliance extends to regional agricultural exports—cotton in Chad, Burkina Faso, and Sudan, groundnuts in Senegal, cocoa in Ghana and Equatorial Guinea, tobacco in Malawi—and to domestic production of wheat, millet, and cassava.

Debt also puts a restriction on economic development in sub-Saharan Africa. In the 1980s and 1990s the region paid a total $170 billion on servicing its overseas debts, a sum four times greater than the health and educa-

tion budget for the whole of southern Africa. So quickly did interest on the initial debt accrue, however, that by 1997 it was three times what it had been in 1980, $235.4 billion, compared with $84.3 billion, despite the money that had been paid back.

International debt handicaps economic development in debtor countries but also brings little long-term benefit to creditor countries. Radical solutions to the problem include the so-called Jubilee 2000 proposal to cancel the deficits to encourage large-scale investment by developed nations that would benefit all parties.

Case study: South Africa

In 1994 the Republic of South Africa held its first free elections and thus signaled the end of apartheid, the institutionalized form of racial segregation under which the country had been ruled for 46 years. Subsequent developments in the newly democratic South Africa have been of particular interest to economists as the country tries to reestablish economic growth after a long period of stagnation.

South Africa's traditional economic ties have been with Britain, which accounts for more than 40 percent of direct foreign investment. The United States comes in a distant second with 15 percent. Nevertheless, the United States is easily the republic's biggest trading partner. During the seven years of sanctions against apartheid 212 U.S. companies pulled out of South Africa, more than from all other countries combined. Since 1994 U.S. involvement has increased again to make it South Africa's largest overseas investor, accounting for $540 million of the $2.2 billion generated in 1998. Bilateral trade, mostly in minerals and machinery, climbed from $4.2 million to $6.7 million over the same period.

Today it is the private sector rather than the U.S. government that is leading the way in investment, putting its faith in a nation

with abundant and diverse resources—gold (33 percent of world production), chromium (29 percent), manganese (16 percent), diamonds (10 percent), and uranium (5 percent)—plus fine agricultural land and enormous potential for tourism. American companies like Dow Chemical, Ford, General Motors, Hyatt, and SBC Communications seem to fear no serious repercussions following the retirement of charismatic President Nelson Mandela in June 1999 and his succession by Thabo Mbeki.

Some observers feel that this confidence is misplaced and regard South Africa as a time bomb. It has an economy smaller than that of Norway but a population ten times larger, of which three-quarters are black and many desperately poor. Skeptics argue that there has been little fundamental social change or redistribution of wealth since the end of apartheid, and that while the white minority continues to hold the reins of economic if not political power, investment is a high-risk strategy because of a possible black backlash. Conversely, if the government strips whites of their disproportionate ownership of capital and land, there will be an exodus of the old guard and a depletion of crucial funds, as occurred with disastrous consequences in neighboring Zimbabwe.

ABOVE: Nelson Mandela, the first president of a truly democratic South Africa. Will the republic remain stable after his retirement?

Latin America

In 1997 Latin America accounted for 8.8 percent of world GDP, almost twice the contribution of the former Soviet bloc. More than 25 percent of all Latin American exports went to the United States, and they provided 15.6 percent of the U.S. market. That same year the region as a whole grew at an overall 5 percent, with Argentina, the Dominican Republic, Guyana, Mexico, and Peru attaining 7 percent growth and Chile 6 percent.

In the past many of the region's economies suffered from political instability, high inflation, and weak banking systems. Following a crisis in the 1980s, most Latin American countries restructured their financial systems, closing banks and introducing strict fiscal policies to reduce inflation. In 1997 Brazil, Argentina, and Mexico were among the world's 20 biggest economies, and most foreign fund managers concentrated their Latin American investments on those three nations plus Chile. Of the other markets investors saw Venezuela and Peru as economically immature, Colombia as vulnerable to the drug trade, Peru as politically unstable, and Bolivia and Paraguay as too poor.

The region's economy remains vulnerable to upheaval, not least that caused by a series of natural disasters: in 1997 Ecuador and Peru were damaged by severe weather associated with the El Niño phenomenon, in 1998 Hurricane Mitch battered Guatemala and Honduras, and at the end of 1999 Venezuela was devastated by floods.

Facing economic crisis

The region also suffered from spillover from the 1998 crisis in East Asia, exacerbated by the fact that some Latin American economies rely on a few commodities: bananas in the Central American isthmus between the Pacific Ocean and the Caribbean; oil in Venezuela; coffee in Colombia; copper in Chile. The East Asian crisis damaged the region's growth and balance of payments through its effect on trade (*see* page 35). While weak East Asian growth and currencies led to lower export volumes, there was a fall in commodity prices and a consequent deterioration in terms of trade.

Most countries in the region introduced appropriate preventive measures by devaluing their currencies and raising their interest rates. Nevertheless, financial flows to Latin America slowed, and lenders began to demand higher

ABOVE: Apart from copper, wine is one of Chile's most profitable exports. This photograph shows a vintner tasting her grapes during the February harvest at the Vina Caliterra vineyard south of the Chilean capital, Santiago.

interest-rate spreads. Trade effects were substantial in Chile, Peru, and Venezuela, which all faced a reduction in the volume and price of their commodity exports, and were particularly significant in Colombia and Mexico.

Crisis in Brazil

The crisis hit most acutely in Brazil, the region's biggest economy and a nation only finally stabilizing after suffering hyperinflation in the early 1990s. The government of the world's eighth-biggest economy, massively in debt, raised interest rates and tightened fiscal policy. These measures would probably have been sufficient to stave off crisis had not Brazil suffered a second blow in the summer of 1998.

This time the cause of the upheaval was financial crisis in Russia, a country with few direct contacts in Latin America. The phenomenon of globalization was amply demonstrated as Russia's collapse persuaded worried foreign banks and money managers to take their money out of Brazil. In January 1999, after capital had flowed out of the country for

BELOW: Poverty is Brazil's greatest and most abiding socioeconomic problem. This photograph shows some of the country's street children asleep on the sidewalk next to multiple television screens.

months, Brazil finally devalued its currency, the real. Experts predicted a return to high inflation and a domino effect in the region to which Argentina and Venezuela would be especially vulnerable. Partly because of U.S. Treasury action, however, the markets responded calmly. By September, with Brazilian inflation running at only 5 percent, investment specialists in London and New York were predicting an economic rebound.

The crisis may well have the effect of stabilizing Latin America's most volatile economy. Overall the region's economy looks healthier than at any time in the continent's history. Hikes in the price of oil and copper have benefited Venezuela and Mexico on one hand and Chile on the other, the world's largest producer of the metal. Now largely free of repressive dictatorships and destructive divisions between U.S.-backed regimes and communist guerrillas, the region is politically stable. Its main problems will probably come from natural disasters, such as those caused by hurricanes and other phenomena associated with El Niño.

The former Soviet bloc

In 1989 the communist governments of many East European countries collapsed in the face of popular demands for the introduction of more democratic forms of government. In 1991 the Soviet Union itself was formally disbanded, restoring independence to its constituent republics, of which the largest and most powerful was the Russian Federation. The Cold War, the long ideological battle between capitalism and communism since World War II, had ended in victory for democracy and the capitalist market.

Some of the economies of Eastern Europe had already made steps toward incorporating elements of a capitalist economy. Hungary, Poland, Czechoslovakia, and Yugoslavia had taken steps under communist government to balance the planned economies' usual emphasis on heavy industry with the development of a consumer sector and export markets. Following the collapse of communism, however, Yugoslavia's economic potential was undermined by the wars that broke out among its constituent republics. Czechoslovakia, too, had its progress restrained by its partition into two independent countries, the Czech Republic and Slovakia. The reunification of East and West Germany, meanwhile, failed initially to solve the problem of the disproportionate distribution of wealth between the capitalist west and the excommunist east.

For most inhabitants of the newly independent states of the former Soviet Union,

Case study: The Andean drugs trade

The laws of economics do not apply only to legitimate forms of commerce. Drug trafficking is an illegal, black market activity that does not appear in national income accounts, but which is nevertheless a major revenue earner. Drugs are a classic example of a demerit good, the use of which creates large negative externalities (costs to society). The externalities in the case of drugs might include increased robbery, as addicts seek money to finance their habit, and hospital treatment when they become sick.

Another significant negative externality is the cost of law enforcement as governments strive to stamp out the drugs trade. The U.S. Drug Enforcement Agency (DEA) is particularly occupied by its attempts to stem the flow of cocaine into America from the Andean region of northwest South America. Nearly all the world's cocaine originates from Bolivia, Peru, or Colombia. In 1995 the 715 metric tons produced in Bolivia and Peru represented 90 percent of the world total, the remaining 10 percent being made in Colombia. Most of the world's cocaine is still produced by the major Colombian drug trafficking groups. They import base cocaine from Peru and Bolivia, process it at secret laboratories in Colombia, and then export it to the U.S. and Europe.

Coffee is Colombia's most important official export, accounting for around half of all revenues, but cocaine is now the country's biggest source of foreign exchange. Violent confrontations between rival gangs and between producers and the authorities occur almost daily. Murders of police officers, judges, civil servants, or anyone investigating the multimillionaire drug barons are commonplace.

In 1990, as part of President George Bush's $10.6 billion "war on drugs," the governments of the three Andean states—Bolivia, Peru, and Colombia—joined forces with the DEA in a concerted effort to smash cocaine production and distribution, notably by trying to break the socioeconomic stranglehold of the drug cartels. While early results in Bolivia were encouraging, the policy in Colombia seemed destined for failure as producers stayed one jump ahead of the authorities.

In 1995 the three governments took new steps against the drug trade. Successes included the arrest or surrender of seven of the eight top drug mafia leaders based in Cali, Colombia, and an assertive campaign against the air bridge between Peru and Colombia. However, these counterdrug initiatives accelerated the trend toward decentralization of the trade and compelled traffickers to change the way they operate. It may well also have made future detection more difficult as the industry has fragmented into hundreds of smaller enterprises and "cells" that employ new trafficking routes.

Drug-trafficking organizations in Mexico were quick to exploit the new situation by expanding direct trade with Peru and Bolivia. The major groups in Mexico are now second only to the Colombian cartels, and trade has shifted as the drug lords of the "Mexican Federation" start to bypass Colombia.

Although it is illegal in virtually every country in the world, the drugs trade is nevertheless a clear illustration of the law of supply and demand. While demand in the developed countries remains high, there will always be producers willing to take risks to get rich, and farmers will continue to grow lucrative plants instead of conventional crops.

In addition to their attempts to intercept smuggled drugs and reduce the amount manufactured—measures that, if successful, will push prices up—governments also finance public awareness campaigns to discourage consumption, lower demand, and thus drive prices down. None of these strategies appears to work on a long-term basis, however.

LEFT: At El Dorado Airport, Bogota, a policeman arrests a man on suspicion of trying to smuggle large quantities of cocaine from Colombia into Mexico.

meanwhile, the transition to a free market was painful. Such was the case in the Baltic states—Estonia, Latvia, and Lithuania—which had been thought to have the best immediate chances of emulating Western European capitalist economies; in the five Asian republics, including the old Soviet "breadbasket" of Kazakhstan; the war-torn Eurasian territories of Armenia, Azerbaijan, and Georgia; and Ukraine, the largest independent country entirely in Europe.

Between 1990 and 1996 standards of living fell in all 15 former Soviet republics, all of which numbered among the 25 nations with the slowest economic growth in the period. The republics all registered an economic contraction between that of Georgia, at –26.1 percent, and Uzbekistan, at –3.5 percent.

Most significantly the list included Russia itself. The world's largest nation by area, for 45 years a nuclear superpower, was recording an annual negative growth of around 9 percent. A cultured country with a long history, sophisticated military technology, and a space exploration program, rich in almost every natural resource, Russia ranked economically behind the Netherlands, Spain, and South Korea.

More freedom, less work

For Russians and most other people of the former Soviet Union the transition from state control to capitalism and the free market was a painful process. Communist corruption and full employment were replaced by free-market economics and welfare lines. The consumer shortages associated with the Soviet years actually grew worse.

Meanwhile, Western entrepreneurs moved to exploit Russia's potential market. Russian businesspeople had neither the financial capital or the market experience to compete. Most indigenous successes were confined to the economic fringe: fashion, fast-food outlets, computers, entertainment, and crime.

From the mid-1990s, however, the economies of the new republics began to show significant signs of improvement, with ten of them growing at a rate of 5 percent or more in 1997. Most had made considerable progress overcoming the initial challenges of transition. By establishing macroeconomic stability, liberalizing markets, and privatizing assets, while maintaining social safety nets in the form of welfare provision, they started to follow the pattern set by the more successful countries of Eastern Europe. Estonia joined

ABOVE: *After the collapse of communism and the breakup of the Soviet Union, many Russians had to come to terms with levels of poverty unseen for 50 years. Here, citizens of St. Petersburg are reduced to selling their belongings in the street.*

Poland, the Czech Republic, Hungary, and Slovenia in formal talks for admission to the European Union; Bulgaria, Latvia, Lithuania, Romania, and Slovakia began longer-term negotiations for future entry.

Russia itself showed signs of hope, recording in 1997 its first growth in GDP since 1989, though only 0.8 percent, and optimistic commentators spoke of a potential boom. Instead 1998 brought bust, with the collapse of the ruble in the summer.

How could a country the size of Russia, with its massive resources and skilled workforce, perform so poorly for so long? The answer lies in two linked areas: the hangovers from the old communist system and the failure to introduce genuine capitalism. Nearly 70 percent of Russian GDP was accounted for by the private sector in 1997, but the failure to dismantle the instruments of central planning quickly and effectively—as had happened in Hungary, for example—proved fatal.

The virtual economy

Even in 1997, the year of Russia's best economic performance since the breakup of the Soviet Union, federal spending was 18.3 percent of GDP, but revenues were only 10.8 percent. The Russian leaders were confronted by the macroeconomic problems of low revenue and high deficit. Despite a successful application by President Boris Yeltsin to join the G7 countries, Russia—unlike most of the other former Soviet republics—did not enter the real world of market forces. The result has been dubbed Russia's "virtual economy."

The root of the problem is that Russia is still failing to produce what the market wants. Industry continues to churn out poor-quality products that nobody can afford. As *Time* magazine put it: "In Soviet times, workers joked that they pretended to work and the state pretended to pay them. Now the line could be that the workers pretend to make things and the factories pretend to sell them."

Reasons for decline

Russia also faced problems with its balance of trade. While more than 60 percent of export earnings in 1997 were derived from the sale of oil and natural gas, more than three-quarters of products sold in the stores of the big cities of European Russia were imported. Russian consumers prefered to buy imported food—about a third of all food eaten—than home-grown produce. The country's output of food fell by 80 percent between 1990 and 1998. In an effort to restore financial balance the West's former enemy borrowed vast amounts of its money and produce, with the International Monetary Fund (IMF) agreeing to substantial aid and loan packages.

A host of interrelated factors contributed to Russia's decline—the sheer size of the country and poor communications among regions, the shortage of corporate business skills, international debts, an inadequate banking system, and the vast sums of money committed to the military budget. The government remained hog-tied by a cumbersome, bureaucratic system. The country's leaders—a Moscow-based clique under a manipulative president—clung to red tape left over from the Soviet period. They seemed incapable of significant action, let alone of the innovation that was needed. The half-hearted transition to capitalism was chaotic in the extreme.

Crash landing

A crash became inevitable, and when it came, the effects were disastrous. In 1998 Russian inflation ran at 84.4 percent, while net foreign direct investment was estimated at only $2.2 billion. The ruble was devalued. Midway through 1999 real disposable incomes had fallen by 26 percent, and some 55 million Russians—more than one-third of the population—were on incomes below the official subsistence level. The Russian Central Bank's reserves stood at $11.8 billion, equivalent to only about 60 percent of the amount needed to service the country's outstanding external debt. Total GDP was running at little more than half its levels in 1989 under Mikhail Gorbachev.

ABOVE: Beneath the glass roof of GUM, the state department store in Red Square, Moscow. In Russia the hoped for economic boom of the post-Communist era has failed to materialize—shortages remain, and there is little consumer confidence.

The fall of the ruble

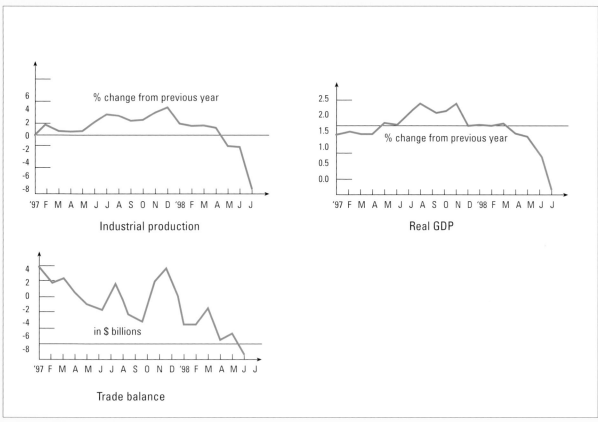

Industrial production

Real GDP

Trade balance

Figure 7 The major indicators of Russia's financial health, from February 1997 to July 1998.

The collapse of the Russian ruble in the summer of 1998 was a timely demonstration of the fact that we now live in a global market as well as a warning of how an economic chill in one country may cause sneezing right across the world.

It all began when the Russian currency was devalued. This in itself was not necessarily disastrous—many economists had been pushing for a small adjustment to support mild economic recovery. But the scale of the resulting drop—34 percent—together with the Russian government's failure to present a convincing short-term package of wide-ranging economic safety measures soon sent the ruble plummeting. Investors rushed to pull out, the panic spread, and the markets closed down. Banks collapsed, the street

value of the ruble halved, and the price of goods rocketed. The crash sent shockwaves around the world. While financier George Soros alone lost $2 billion, much of Latin America also suffered badly—Brazil was worst hit—and nearly 500 points were knocked off the Dow Jones in New York. Prompt action by the U.S. Treasury helped avert panic, but fears grew over the delicate health of many other former Soviet republics, whose economies remained closely linked with Russia. Coming in the wake of the East Asian crash of the previous summer, the ruble disaster forced many governments and corporations to reassess their international investment strategies, which no longer included Russia.

RIGHT: Russian President Boris Yeltsin, whose policies contributed to the collapse of the ruble in 1998.

In theory, at least, Russia is one of the world's richest nations. It holds 36 percent of the planet's known natural-gas reserves and 13 percent of its oil; its gold and diamond reserves are among top three in the world, and it has supplies of almost every important mineral, plus vast coniferous forests.

Yet foreign governments and individuals are now extremely reluctant to invest in this huge and wealthy country. After the breakup of the Soviet Union Western nations pumped tens of billions of dollars into Russia in the expectation of political and infrastructural changes that never happened and in support of reforms that were never implemented. These disappointed investors would now inevitably look elsewhere—to Latin America, perhaps, or parts of Africa—leaving the largest country on earth licking its economic wounds and dangerously isolated.

The international threat, however, is less real than the prospect of domestic chaos. The Russian people—fed for centuries on a diet of privation and false promises—faced the aftermath of the 1998 crash with characteristic calm and stoicism. But even they have limits to their endurance. The costly struggles for independence in Chechnya and Dagestan may be just a taste of the tribulations to come.

Acting unpaid officers

Whole sectors of the Russian workforce—from soldiers fighting dissidents in the Caucasus to coalminers in the industrial Urals—regularly go without pay for months. While many older citizens hanker after a return to the safety nets

of their Soviet past, young people grow frustrated by the government's failure to deliver the fruits of capitalism. To add to their frustration, Russians witness the material rewards they crave being reaped with relative ease by several of their former satellite states in Eastern Europe.

The future course of the Russian economy is uncharted and will remain so for as long as the government continues to be so politically mercurial. President Boris Yeltsin proved an autocratic, czarlike leader who effectively prevented economic progress. On December 31, 1999, however, he announced that he would step down and nominated as his successor the prime minister, Vladimir Putin. Although some observers were wary of Putin's Russian nationalist stance—visible particularly in his support for the military assault on the breakaway republic of Chechnya—he promised to bring the stability his predecessor had failed to deliver.

Europe

Although the United States is the world's leading single nation in economic terms, even its performance is outstripped by the combined resources and output of the European Community (EC) and the European Free Trade Association (EFTA). The EC is an alliance of 15 nations that in 1997 contained 370 million people and accounted for almost 20 percent of the world's total GDP, making it in economic terms well over twice the size of Latin America and nearly three times bigger

ABOVE: An armored personnel carrier abandoned on the outskirts of Vladivostok, Russia. Military spending was one of the first items of government expenditure to be cut after the collapse of the ruble.

The Aral Sea: lake of tears

Since the fall of communism Russia and other former nations of the Soviet Union have been criticized for their failure—through lack of money and political will—to make good the damage caused by the old regime to the environment: what economists term unwanted externalities. Few Soviet undertakings were as ill-conceived as the one that attempted to divert the waters of the Amudarya and Syrdarya—two major rivers of Central Asia—from the Aral Sea, into which they naturally flowed, to irrigate the production of cotton, wheat, and rice in the steppes and semi-deserts of Kazakhstan, Uzbekistan, and Turkmenistan. By this method the irrigated area was more than doubled between 1950 and 1990, transforming 27,000 arid square miles into fertile land.

But the cost of this development was immeasurable. Starved of more than half its source water, the world's fourth biggest lake shrank to nearly a third of its original area and 35 percent of its former volume as it dried up into three almost separate sections. The high rate of evaporation increased salinity threefold, making the waters as salty as the oceans and killing all 24 indigenous species of fish. The fishing industry, which had thrived on catches of 40,000 tons a year until 1960, disappeared. The shoreline is abandoned, and vessels lie rusting in salty bogs.

The environmental damage did not end there. High levels of pollutants from the pesticides, defoliants, and fertilizers used on the cotton and grain fields found their way back into the rivers, further denuding the Aral Sea, contaminating local groundwater supplies, and seriously affecting health in the area. In 1989 infant mortality rates there were four times the Soviet average.

Even the benefits were short-lived. Large bodies of water have a mediating effect on local climates. The shrinkage of the Aral Sea set in motion a powerful meteorological reaction that brought higher summer temperatures of up to 113°F (45°C). In the wake of this came greater aridity, which reduced humidity levels by nearly 30 percent and desertified an area stretching hundreds of miles from the shore. This defeated the original object of the exercise—in most areas around the Aral Sea it has now become too dry to grow cotton.

The initial cost-benefit analysis took little account of crucial environmental factors. Driven by an unstoppable desire in Moscow to make the Soviet Union self-sufficient in cotton, it ignored warnings of the possible consequences. Now the independent states—already among some of the poorer nations—are faced with an almost insoluble problem. Improved conservation and care of water resources are the short-term priorities, but the wider climatic changes can be reversed only if the Aral Sea is restored to something like its former scale.

The ambitious plans, first drawn up in the 1970s, to divert water some 1,500 miles from giant north-flowing rivers in western Siberia would now involve the cooperation of Russia and the three Asian republics. The scheme is daunting also because of the possible environmental repercussions, from the cooling of the Arctic Ocean to the spread of waterborne parasites in the south.

For the foreseeable future it appears that this once fertile ecosystem will remain a toxic wasteland. As one prominent Uzbek poet put it: "You cannot fill the Aral with tears."

ABOVE: In the newly arid parts of the Aral Sea, the only ships that can work their passage are ships of the desert.

than Japan. The members of EFTA are Iceland, Norway, and Switzerland, which is the world's richest country in per capita terms.

At the dawn of the 21st century, with Japan locked in recession, Southeast Asia in crisis, Russia in long-term decline, and Latin America still politically unsettled, Europe's economic role had become pivotal to the world economy. Even though European Community trade has tended to become more internalized—in 1997 more than 60 percent took place among members—the influence on investments and markets of its four most prominent nations (Germany, France, Italy, and the United Kingdom) is still crucial to the world economy.

The success of Europe's performance in the 1990s has been achieved only with a considerable degree of social, political, and financial upheaval. While Germany has been the driving force for European economic integration, it was the United Kingdom that set the pattern of deregulatory economic change on the U.S. model. Successive U.K. governments reduced the level of state control, created flexible money and labor markets, and encouraged the development of a society based on greater individual choice.

Conservative estimates

In the 1980s Britain's Conservative Party launched a twin attack on what it perceived as the two greatest obstacles to economic progress: nationalized industries and strong labor unions. Under prime ministers Margaret Thatcher and John Major they all but vanished between 1979 and 1997. The post-1997 Labour government maintained similar policies.

For many in Britain the revolution was painful because the economy underwent two recessions before apparently breaking the cycle of boom and bust. In the early 1990s, as the continental countries sank into recession, the United Kingdom emerged at the forefront of new enterprise. Most of Europe followed the British example of deregulation, and by

LEFT: On this map of Europe the members of the European Union are colored pink; the members of the European Free Trade Association are colored gold.

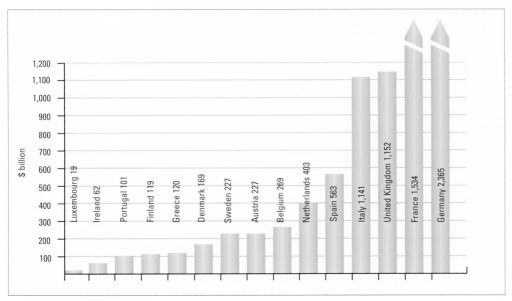

Figure 8 The GDPs of the European Union countries in 1997.

1997 the EU as a whole had established a relatively stable pattern of steady but modest growth, low inflation, single-figure interest rates, controlled inflation, and sustainable levels of unemployment.

Patterns of growth

Among the mature and complex economies of the EC the precise pattern of national growth is bound to vary. In Britain deregulation has created a pool of skilled, deunionized, and comparatively cheap labor that has helped attract record high levels of investment from foreign manufacturers, such as East Asian car makers. From 1996 to 1998 the United Kingdom earned more from these sources than all other EC members combined. Critics of the new-look U.K. economy say that such an arrangement allows profits to flow abroad.

Germany—for many years touted as a model economy—was hard hit by the cost of reunification in 1990 and the resulting unemployment rate of 10 percent. But the nation has managed to sustain respectable growth rates throughout the remainder of the decade. France, despite continued attempts to broaden its industrial base, remains strongly influenced by its agriculture. Many French farmers fear that the new Eastern European applicants for EC membership—many of which also have largely rural populations—will damage their interests by taking out more in grants than they will put in to the community.

The EC grew slowly at first. The six original signatories of the Treaty of Rome (1957)—Belgium, France, Germany, Luxembourg, Italy, and the Netherlands—were gradually joined by another nine nations, three of

LEFT: In 1997 Tony Blair became the first Labour prime minister of Britain since 1979. Many of his economic policies were either identical to—or a logical development of—those of his Conservative predecessors.

Birth pains of a new European currency

On January 1, 1999, the euro became the official currency of 11 of the 15 member states of the European Community, with a fixed conversion rate against all their national currencies. As with any other unit, the value of the euro against the U.S. dollar and all other currencies—including those of the four members that still remain outside the Euro Zone—may now rise and fall depending on market conditions.

Although euro notes and coins will not appear until January 1, 2002, the new currency can already be used in the form of checks, travelers' checks, bank transfers, and credit cards. The participating countries are (in descending order of size of economy) Germany, France, Italy, Spain, the Netherlands, Belgium, Austria, Finland, Portugal, Ireland, and Luxembourg.

The introduction of the new currency is an unprecedented response to the increased globalization of the world economy. According to the European Commission, it "confirms the advent of a genuine culture of stability in Europe that is essential to the establishment of a stable, sound, and efficiently managed economic framework… Economic and monetary union (EMU) will revitalize the European economy and the single market, foster investment, boost business competitiveness, benefit savers, and make life easier for citizens where both work and travel are concerned."

While all this is the logical culmination of the European Monetary Union (EMU) process, it is still a revolutionary step in economic history for so many nations voluntarily to bind themselves together so intimately. As the economist David Shukman has pointed out: "Europeans have only previously witnessed a single currency when it was forced on them—under the Roman Empire and Hitler's Third Reich."

There are many economic advantages to such a cooperative venture. The removal of currency-exchange costs will enable companies to make big savings, while businesses will no longer suffer loss of profits due to the volatility of exchange rates. In 2002, however, there will be a more tangible, political aspect to the change—each nation will have a national symbol on its money, but the euro will be the common currency for all citizens. After three years of electronic use the euro will become a constant reminder to people that they are fully paid-up Europeans.

Economic milestone

The euro is intended to be a third major global currency, alongside the U.S. dollar and the Japanese yen. Indeed, in terms of the share of world GDP output the combined weight of the member economies is more than twice that of Japan and within hailing distance of that of the United States.

ABOVE: If euros like these prove as successful as the EC hopes, national coins and notes may become relics of a bygone age.

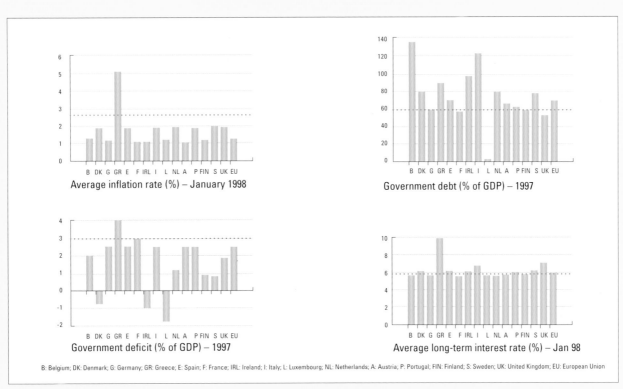

Average inflation rate (%) – January 1998

Government debt (% of GDP) – 1997

Government deficit (% of GDP) – 1997

Average long-term interest rate (%) – Jan 98

B: Belgium; DK: Denmark; G: Germany; GR: Greece; E: Spain; F: France; IRL: Ireland; I: Italy; L: Luxembourg; NL: Netherlands; A: Austria; P: Portugal; FIN: Finland; S: Sweden; UK: United Kingdom; EU: European Union

Figure 9 The convergence criteria for joining the euro, with required levels indicated by the dotted red line.

The European Commission claims that "the euro will gradually come to be one of the world's leading transaction, investment, and reserve currencies. It will demonstrate the existence and the unity of Europe to its partners and will help to make the international monetary system more stable."

The commission's use of the word "gradually" is significant. Few neutral observers felt that the euro would replace its component parts in world markets, and indeed the new currency took a beating against the U.S. dollar its in first few months on the foreign exchange markets. Its image as a "virtual currency" raised serious doubts about its long-term viability, despite its early success in Europe.

Although there were concerns about possible hitches, the complex changeover to the new currency went smoothly enough. The European Central Bank, set up in Frankfurt as part of the EMU process, reported that transactions between member states soon reached over a trillion dollars a day, close to U.S. levels.

In Europe the euro made its biggest impact on the bond market. In the first three months after its debut the issue of new bonds reached $240 billion, almost 25 percent more than the U.S. total. Another effect has been the increase in the number of cross-border mergers due to the removal of the currency risk previously involved. Meanwhile, the low inflation rates demanded for membership in the EMU has stimulated investment across the board, and especially in large blue-chip companies, a natural target for international investment in an immature market.

The Maastricht Treaty of 1991 laid down five criteria for good economic management. They were the targets countries would have to meet in order to qualify for European Monetary Union. The four significant standards were average inflation rate (reference value 2.7 percent), average long-term interest rate (7.8 percent), government deficit as a percentage of GDP (3 percent), and government debt as percentage of GDP (60 percent). These tests led to an unseemly scrambling of policies in some countries as governments strove to find ways of meeting the targets. Privatization proceeds were boosted by "creative accounting"; debt was relieved by selling off gold reserves; Italy even raised a special "euro tax." There were suspicions, too, as second-tier nations suddenly recorded exceptionally good figures. The average general government deficit in the community fell sharply from 6.1 percent of GDP in 1993 to a comfortable 2.4 percent in 1997.

Sweden and Greece failed to meet the criteria—Sweden on government debt, Greece on all four counts—while Denmark and the U.K. decided against entry in the first wave. British prime minister Tony Blair followed the cautious policy of his predecessor, John Major, keeping the U.K. economy—the community's third largest—outside the euro zone until after a general election that will take place by 2002.

British reservations about monetary union—which, according to opinion polls, are shared increasingly by most continental countries—do not rest solely on fears of losing sovereignty. The policy-makers of the community—especially the commission and the central bank— are unelected; there is widespread waste and proven corruption; tax harmonization seems an almost unachievable fiscal goal. Britain's fence-sitting may be controversial, unpopular, and even dangerous. But it is a strategy that, like the euro itself, can be assessed only in the longer term.

which—Sweden, Finland, and Austria—defected from EFTA in 1995.

On March 30, 1998, the EC formally launched a program of admissions that, when completed, will increase membership to 26. The first wave of new members, the so-called "fast-track membership," comprised large and small Central and Eastern European countries—the Czech Republic, Estonia, Hungary, Poland, and Slovenia—together with the island of Cyprus in the Mediterranean Sea. The applications of the second batch of hopefuls—Bulgaria, Latvia, Lithuania, Slovakia, and Romania—have been processed more slowly because their less-developed economies need longer to satisfy the criteria for entry.

This long process may well focus attention on perennial conflicts over EC funding. Large EC grants effectively use contributions from richer nations to subsidize poorer ones. All the applicants have poorer economies than the current EC members, who will strive to safeguard their own interests. Nations that have been receiving substantial EC grants—notably Ireland, Portugal, and Spain—will not want to see these valuable funds diverted eastward, while no member country wants to increase its contribution to the kitty.

The Common Agricultural Policy, a system of grants that accounts for nearly half the total EC budget, is already under strain, and several applicants have farming economies that desperately need financial support. New member countries hoping for an instant rise in their standard of living may well be disappointed.

Many EC members are concerned about what they regard as needless expansion. They take the view that bigger is not necessarily better and that an increase from 15 to 26 nations will only serve to weaken the community. The organization will merely be importing intractable problems from Eastern Europe and the unstable Balkan peninsula. More members will also complicate the decision-making process within the community.

If European integration is achieved, it is more likely to be through the development of a

single currency (see box, page 90) than through political unity. Although the EC has already achieved some economic and financial synthesis there is little evidence to suggest that the member states will agree any real common foreign policy. This was borne out by their squabbling in 1999 over whether to take military action against Serbia in the Serb province of Kosovo. Most EC citizens currently enjoy a high standard of living, and antiexpansionists argue that this will be maintained only if the community confines itself to doing what, until now, it appears to have done relatively well.

LEFT: French farmers benefit from EC subsidies and have a long history of industrial action. In June 1992 they picketed Disneyland, Paris, to protest EC expansion.

SEE ALSO:

• Volume 3, page 6: Government and the economy

• Volume 5, page 6: Balance of payments

• Volume 5, page 25: The developing world

• Volume 5, page 36: Externalities, environmental

• Volume 5, page 53: International debt

• Volume 5, page 75: Multinational corporations

• Volume 6, page 106: Today and tomorrow

BELOW: Representatives of the EC member nations at the signing of the Maastricht Treaty in 1991.

International economic organizations

Since the end of World War II in 1945 the fear of another such conflict has been the strongest of the many motivational forces that have led to the creation of a large number of international organizations dedicated to the maintenance of a stable world economy.

The 20th century's two world wars caused a breakdown in international trade that was catastrophic for the development of the world economy. The years between the outbreak of World War I in 1914 and the end of World War II in 1945 provided overwhelming evidence that peace and prosperity were inseparable. Economists and politicians therefore resolved to do all they could to ensure that the main trading nations became so closely interdependent that such large-scale and wide-ranging hostilities would henceforth be impossible. This chapter looks at some of the organizations that have since been created to help achieve that objective.

Never again

The Wall Street Crash of 1929 and the economic hardships of the world recession that followed it stimulated serious debate about the global economy and how, if possible, it could be managed in such a way as to eliminate the risk of it failing again. World War II, with its huge cost in lives, resources, and money, determined the Allies—particularly the United States, the United Kingdom, and France—to prevent another global conflict of such magnitude. The British economist John Maynard Keynes had rightly predicted that the reparation payments demanded from the Germans to pay for World War I would sow the seeds for a second major conflict. The recession and accompanying hyperinflation in 1930s Germany left a demoralized nation half-starving and created an environment ideally suited for the growth of the Nazi Party under Adolf Hitler.

Even before 1945, when the Allies achieved victory in Europe and the Pacific, detailed plans were being made to set up a new world order based on discussion and consensus rather than on mutual mistrust and the ever-present threat of armed conflict. The

ABOVE: New recruits flock to join the Nazi Party in Munich, Germany, in 1935. The war and atrocities that followed the rise of Hitler made the world determined to ensure that it never saw the like again.

LEFT: A pedestrian in Auckland, New Zealand, walks past a wall covered with photographs of some of the world's political prisoners. This collage was put up by activists who want to see human rights form part of the APEC agenda, which is currently preoccupied exclusively with economic matters.

United Nations, the World Bank, and the International Monetary Fund (IMF), for example, all owe their foundation to the strength of the worldwide will to end war.

The Bretton Woods Conference

As World War II came to an end, 44 representatives of the United States and other allied countries met at the New Hampshire resort of Bretton Woods to establish a new world monetary system. Their main aim was to eliminate the fluctuations in international exchange rates, and to this end, they restored the gold standard for the U.S. dollar. Gold was then valued at $35 per ounce. The other countries agreed to fix (peg) their exchange rates to the U.S. dollar (*see* The U.S. government and world economics, page 6).

This key element of fixed exchange rates, however, began to fail in the 1960s, when most countries shifted toward floating exchange rates. But floating exchange rates led to financial indiscipline, economic stagnation, and the creation of rampant inflation throughout the world.

To facilitate the fixing of exchange rates, the IMF and the World Bank were set up in 1947 to help the many countries, particularly in Europe, that were still in crisis after World War II. The creation in 1948 of the General Agreement on Tariffs and Trade (GATT)—now the World Trade Organization (WTO) (see page 114)—was also intended to gradually ease the barriers to international trade.

These institutions are still in place, with greatly increased membership. The specific aims and internal composition of these and other important international trade organizations are described below.

Asia-Pacific Economic Cooperation (APEC)

The APEC group was formed in Canberra, Australia, in 1989 in response to the growing interdependence among the economies of the Pacific Rim. Initially an informal consultative forum, APEC has developed into the primary vehicle for economic cooperation and the promotion of trade in the Asia-Pacific region. APEC is also crucial in global terms, with its 21 members currently accounting for nearly one-half of world trade.

APEC was formally established at a meeting in 1992 in Bangkok, Thailand. Its permanent secretariat is now located in Singapore. The first meeting of heads of government took place at Seattle, Washington, in the following year, and since then each annual meeting of APEC foreign and economic ministers has been followed by an informal gathering of APEC leaders at which common policy objectives have been discussed.

The initial APEC meeting in 1989 was between the six members of ASEAN—Brunei, Indonesia, Malaysia, the Philippines, Singapore, and Thailand—and six dialogue partners. When Peru, Russia, and Vietnam joined in 1998, it took the membership of APEC to 21. The other members are Australia, Canada, Chile, China (originally also Hong Kong), Japan, South Korea, Mexico, New Zealand, Papua New Guinea, Taiwan, and the United States.

Aims and activities of APEC

At Seattle in 1993 leaders of the Pacific Rim economies declared their intention to create a community serving mutual interests that was based on a spirit of partnership and openness. Cooperative efforts would be made to solve the challenges of sustainable and sensitive economic growth based on the free exchange of goods, services, and investment.

Liberalization of trade is the key factor in APEC's strategy: at the summit held in Bogor, Indonesia in 1994 it was agreed that the members would work toward the goal of a free trade and investment zone by the year 2020. Later in 1994 two other central pillars of APEC activities were formalized—business facilitation and technical cooperation.

In 1996, at Manila, Philippines, attention focused on six areas to achieve the objectives outlined in Bogor: promoting environmentally sustainable growth, strengthening economic infrastructures, fostering efficient capital markets, encouraging the growth of small and medium-sized enterprises, harnessing progressive technologies, and developing "human capital."

APEC's commitment to cooperative growth strategy was reaffirmed at the meeting in Kuala Lumpur, Malaysia, in 1998, when representatives agreed to strengthen trade and investment flows, economic infrastructures, financial systems, commercial links, safety nets, the scientific and technological base, and human resources development.

During a decade of considerable progress for most of the Pacific Rim the only difficult year was 1997. The Economic Leaders' Meeting was held in Vancouver, Canada, in November of that year, right after an economic crisis that profoundly affected many APEC members. The final declaration of the summit endorsed a framework of measures agreed on by deputy finance ministers and central bank governors at an emergency meeting held in Manila the previous week. Attended by experts from the World Bank, the IMF, and the Asian Development Bank, this meeting urged APEC ministers and governors to speed up efforts to liberalize capital flows in the region and hasten moves to develop its financial and capital markets. Various measures were put in place to expedite these processes. It is widely believed that the existence of APEC helped minimize the effects of the Asian collapse (*see* The U.S. government and world economics, page 6) and may even have averted a world crash.

The Vancouver meeting steadfastly insisted that the instability should not be allowed to hold up the liberalization of trade, and nine economic sectors were identified as early targets—chemicals, energy, environmental goods and services, fish and fish products, forestry products, gems and jewelry, medical equipment and instruments, telecommunications, and toys. APEC also declared its support for an agreement to liberalize financial services, a deal successfully negotiated under the auspices of the WTO the following month.

BELOW: U.S. Vice-President Al Gore with Japan's Prime Minister Tomiichi Murayayama at the APEC summit in Osaka, Japan, November 1995.

Structure and organization

In addition to its Secretariat in Singapore, APEC has five major committees and groups, all of which were set up between 1993 and 1995. They comprise the Agricultural Technical Cooperative Experts Group (ATC), the Budget and Administrative Committee (BAC), the Committee on Trade and Investment (CTI), the Economic Committee, and the Ad Hoc Policy Level Group on Small and Medium Enterprises (PLG-SME).

APEC also uses a system of working groups to implement plans in response to the directives of the economic leaders' meetings. It also promotes technical and practical cooperation in specific areas. Working groups have been set up for energy, fisheries, human resources development (comprising five networks in different spheres of human resources, training, and education), industrial science and technology, marine resource conservation (every APEC member state has a Pacific coastline), telecommunications, tourism, trade and investment data review, trade promotion, and transportation.

The Ministerial Meeting of 1995, held in Osaka, Japan, agreed to establish the APEC Business Advisory Council (ABAC), formed by up to three delegates from the private sector of each member economy. ABAC's role was to accelerate the liberalization of trade, and at its first meeting at Manila in 1996 it agreed to set its sights on infrastructure, regional finance and communications, cross-border investment and human resource development, notably in small- and medium-sized enterprises. Later, in 1998, ABAC concentrated on applying measures to dampen the effects of the financial crisis in southeast Asia.

Bank for International Settlement (BIS)

One of the few surviving international organizations to predate the United Nations, the BIS was forged by the Hague Agreements of 1930. One of its first tasks was to tackle the question of German reparations after World War I. Its wider mission, however, was to promote cooperation among the world's national central banks, to provide facilities for international financial operations and economic research, and—as its name suggests—to act as an agent or trustee in the various international financial settlements that were entrusted to it.

BELOW: This 1930 meeting of European powers to discuss German war reparations at The Hague, Netherlands, led to the formation of the Bank for International Settlement.

Effectively, the BIS now functions as the bank of the important central banks. Its total assets—some $130 billion as at March 31, 1998—are owned by 45 central banks, which are entitled to attend and vote at BIS's annual general meetings. All but 13 of the member countries are in Europe; the rest comprise mainly the world's larger non-European economies—Australia, Brazil, Canada, China, India, Japan, South Korea, Mexico, Saudi Arabia, Singapore, South Africa, and the United States.

The BIS has the legal form of a limited company, but as an international organization governed by international law it also benefits from special immunities and privileges. Initially, the central banks involved were given the option of subscribing the shares or arranging for their subscription inside their own countries, with the result that the BIS has always had some private shareholders. They cannot participate in the annual meeting, however, and they account for only 14 percent of the total share capital—the other 86 percent resides with the central banks.

Structure and organization

The board of BIS is responsible for the conduct of the bank's operations. Its 16 directors are the governors of the central banks of Belgium, Canada, France, Germany, Italy, Japan, Netherlands, Sweden, Switzerland, the United Kingdom, and the United States. Based in Basel, Switzerland, the bank employs nearly 500 staff from 29 countries. In July 1998 BIS set up its first overseas administrative unit, the Representative Office for Asia and the Pacific, operating out of Hong Kong, which was by then an integral part of the People's Republic of China. Since January 1998 the Basel offices have also played host to the secretariat of the International Association of Insurance Supervisors (IAIS), which was originally set up in 1994.

The BIS operates three standing committees. They are the Basel Committee on Banking Supervision, the Committee on the Global Financial System (CGFS), and the Committee on Payment and Settlement Systems (CPSS). A number of groups covering specialized areas have also been established, including one on computers.

In 1998, in response to the economic crises in southeast Asia and Russia, a joint initiative of BIS and the Basel Committee set up the Financial Stability Institute, the aim of which is to strengthen financial systems around the world by encouraging interaction among the central banks, the private sector, and various supervisory authorities. The bank's Monetary and Economic Department

collects data on securities markets and international banking developments, researches a range of monetary and financial issues, and runs a database for the central banks.

Scope and activities

The BIS is responsible for some 7 percent of the world's foreign exchange reserves, and the organization helps central banks manage and invest their monetary reserves. In 1998, 120 central banks and financial institutions had deposits with the organization. Some of these funds are earmarked for lending to other central banks.

The BIS cooperates closely with both the World Bank and the IMF, and participates in meetings of the G10 group of industrialized nations, a major forum for debates about international monetary concerns since it was set up in 1962. A Standing Committee of the G10 central banks was established at the BIS in 1971 to monitor the development of eurocurrency markets. Since 1986 BIS has also acted as agent for the clearing and settlement system of the European currency unit (ecu). In 1994 the bank took on another role as collateral agent in the rescheduling of Brazil's external debt, and it later acted in a similar capacity for Peru in 1997 and the Ivory Coast in the following year.

European Bank for Reconstruction and Development (EBRD)

Founded in May 1990 after the lifting of the Iron Curtain (*see* The world economy, page 63) and inaugurated in April 1991, the EBRD aims to foster and help the transition of the nations of Eastern Europe from centrally planned economies to free-market systems. It lends funds at market rates to countries "committed to, and applying, the fundamental principles of multiparty democracy, pluralism and market economics."

Based in London, England, the bank has 60 members—58 states plus the European Union and the European Investment Bank. Apart from the core European members, membership includes the five former Soviet republics of Central Asia and non-European nations that for historical, geographical, and cultural reasons have special economic ties with the continent of Europe: Australia, Canada, Egypt, Israel, Japan, Mexico, Morocco, New Zealand, South Korea, and the United States.

The biggest subscriber is the United States, which provides the EBRD with 10 percent of its funds, while France, Germany, Italy, the

ABOVE: The headquarters of the European Bank for Reconstruction and Development in Exchange Square, London, England.

United Kingdom, and Japan each account for 8.5 percent. In 1996 total subscriptions to the EBRD reached 20 billion euros; the bank is now also licensed to borrow on world capital markets.

Operations and activities of the EBRD

The EBRD's initial policy statement in May 1991 outlined programs to achieve the following objectives:

● Support existing national infrastructures and encourage the creation of new ones in recently independent countries.

● Bring about the privatization and reform of the financial sector, including the further development of world capital markets and commercial banks.

● Encourage foreign investment.

● Develop the competitive sectors of small and medium-size enterprises in agriculture, industry, and services.

● Restructure industrial sectors on a competitive basis.

● Promote sustainable and environmentally sound development.

The EBRD is thus tasked to finance projects in both the private and the public sectors, although no more than 40 percent of its investment can be made in state-owned concerns. By the end of 1998 over 80 percent of the EBRD's total committed funding for its 551 approved projects was for the private sector.

The largest recipients of EBRD funding are financial services and businesses in transitional economies. The country that receives most is Russia, which accounts for just over a quarter of its banking portfolio, followed by Romania, Hungary, Poland, and Ukraine. The 1998 economic crisis in Russia had a huge impact on EBRD operations, and in October of that year the beleaguered Russian Central Bank asked the EBRD to help with the restructuring of the country's banking system.

Many members, however, questioned the wisdom of allocating such massive amounts of money to Russian banks, which they perceived as something of a lost cause. In January 1999 the bank announced a large-scale program to develop trade between Eastern European countries and the confederation of Independent States (CIS), the body comprising the former Soviet republics, in an attempt to solve the severe economic plight of the region. As well as Russia, the economies of Ukraine and Belarus appeared to many western analysts to be in terminal decline.

The Nuclear Safety Account (NSA)

ABOVE: The 1986 Chernobyl disaster focused the attention of the world on the dangers of nuclear spillage.

In 1993, spurred by fears of a repeat of the Chernobyl nuclear power plant disaster in Ukraine and a host of near-catastrophes caused by lack of adequate finances and supervision, the G7 (now G8) industrialized countries proposed the establishment of a Nuclear Safety Account (NSA), a body that would fund a multilateral program for the improvement of safety in the vulnerable nuclear power plants of the countries of the former Soviet Union.

Administered by the EBRD, the establishment of the NSA was approved by the bank's 24-member board of directors. Almost immediately the European Union earmarked 260 million euros for the NSA, and by the end of 1997 some 14 other countries had also pledged substantial funds. Projects were soon under way to regulate nuclear power stations in Lithuania, Russia, Ukraine, and Bulgaria.

After finance and business, transportation has been the biggest recipient of EBRD funding since 1991, although in 1997 much-needed restructuring of manufacturing marginally outstripped finance and business as transportation fell to fourth place, well behind the energy and power-generation sector. Such changes reflect the shifting requirements and needs of various countries in transition: for example, more than 17 percent of the bank's overall financial commitment in 1997 went to environmental investments.

The bank has to decide between the relative merits of a wide range of possible investments. Funds go to improving municipal services, privatizing and upgrading national telecommunications operators, financing agriculture, fishing, and food processing. The EBRD even monitors progress in the control of corporate corruption. In the CIS examples of EBRD funding include water and sewage in St. Petersburg, an airport in Uzbekistan, and road improvements in Turkmenistan.

The Group of Eight (G8)

Consisting of eight of the world's leading industrial nations—the United States, Japan, Germany, the United Kingdom, France, Italy, Canada, and Russia—the G8 meets on a regular basis to shape and coordinate policies that affect the world economy. In addition to the macroeconomic goals of stabilizing exchange rates, international trade, and monitoring loans to poorer countries, the mandate of the G8 has broadened to include other world issues such as international terrorism, the information superhighway, and the control of

Other G forces

There are several other groups that have been formed on the same basis as the G8. They include:

● G3—this is an informal term applied to the world's three most powerful industrial nations, Germany, Japan, and the United States. (It is also confusingly used for the Latin American oil-exporting countries Colombia, Mexico, and Venezuela.)

● G10—also known as the Paris Club, this group was created in 1962 and included the IMF and nine creditor nations—Belgium, Canada, France, Germany, Italy, Netherlands, Sweden, the United Kingdom, and the United States. Although Japan and Switzerland have since joined, in 1964 and 1984 respectively, it has kept its original title.

● G24—set up in 1972, this group advises the IMF of issues relevant to developing countries. The membership is divided equally between the Americas, Africa, and Asia. It is also the name of the group of 24 industrial countries, derived from OECD countries and chaired by the European Commission, that coordinates aid to Eastern Europe and former Soviet republics.

drug trafficking. Other important concerns, such as the changes in Eastern Europe, the international debt crisis of the 1980s, and payment for the Gulf War, are debated as they arise.

The beginnings of G8

Although G8 came into being only in 1998, it can trace its origins back to 1967. An informal meeting between the finance ministers and governors of the central banks of the then five most powerful nations—France, Germany, Japan, the United Kingdom, and the United States—began what was to become an irregular series of meetings. These meetings developed into regular summits for the member countries' heads of state.

The first of these summits took place at Rambouillet, France, in 1975, when Italy was admitted. The following year in Puerto Rico, Canada joined as the seventh member, and the Group of Seven (G7) was launched. At the London summit of 1977 the European Community was represented, but the name remained G7. Since 1994 Russia has held postsummit meetings with the seven in a grouping known as the Political 8 (P8). The 1998 summit saw Russia fully participate, and the G8 was born, although the G7 continues to function informally.

To help manage many of the issues raised at the summits, there are supporting forums at ministerial level. They have included, for example, discussions of trade (1982), foreign affairs (1984), finance (1986), the environment (1992), and employment (1994). Additional task forces are also formed to tackle specific transnational issues, such as money laundering and the smuggling of illegal immigrants. Often the resolutions require changes in member countries' domestic laws to allow full international cooperation.

The G8, however, also has critics who believe that it can never meet its professed aims. They argue that the task of putting group interests before national interests is too difficult to achieve. Many also agree that since the world money and commodity markets are

ABOVE: World leaders in Cologne, Germany, for the G8 summit in June 1999.

now controlled by traders, the ability of G8 to coordinate world economic policy has been seriously diminished. Economists have also criticized the group for making unthought-out, hasty decisions that are either not put into practice or not properly supervised. Many blame G7 for the worldwide inflation that followed the 1978 summit and for the global stockmarket crash of 1987, which has been attributed to G7's alleged mishandling of exchange rate policy in the mid-1980s.

Inter-American Development Bank (IDB)

The oldest and largest regional development organization, the IDB was set up in 1959 to promote the individual and collective

development of countries in Latin America and the Caribbean. These objectives were achieved by financing economic and social projects and through the provision of technical assistance.

The original IDB membership of 19—Latin American and Caribbean nations plus the United States—had by the end of the century risen to 46. As well as its natural pan-American core, this number comprises 16 European states and two Asian countries, Israel and Japan. Its headquarters are in Washington, D.C., but there are offices in each of the borrowing member states and special offices in Paris, France, and Tokyo. The IDB's administrative budget for 1998 was $371.1 million.

All the powers of the bank are vested in the board of governors, which meets annually. IDB governors are generally ministers of finance, presidents of central banks, or people of comparable status and experience. The United States holds 34.7 percent of the votes on the board, a figure proportional to its stake in the bank's capital.

In 1988 the United States proposed that a majority of 65 percent be required to approve loans, replacing the simple majority system. The developing member states had 54 percent of the votes, and the new proposal would have given the combined vote of the United States and Canada an effective veto. While the new proposal was not accepted, there was agreement in principle on a new system of delaying powers: one shareholder could now delay approval of loans for two months, two could postpone it for another five months, and three (provided that they had 40 percent of the votes) could delay it by another five months. After that, however, approval was still to be decided by a simple majority.

Allocation of funds

In 1997 the IDB borrowed the equivalent of $5.6 billion on the international capital markets, taking its total borrowings outstanding to over $28.6 billion. The same year saw the organization approve 107 loans totaling $6 billion, taking the total since its first loans in 1961 to just over $84 billion. Almost a third of the 1997 loans went to "physical infrastructure" (energy, transport, and communications), while public sector reform and modernization, social investment, urban development, and education each received more than $600 million.

In 1991 the Program for the Development of Technical Cooperation was established, financed by European countries and the European Union. By the end of 1997 the disbursements from this and other trust funds amounted to just over $1.7 billion, covering 205 loans. Two years later a Multilateral Investment Fund was set up to promote private investment, divided into facilities for

ABOVE: The IDB sent funds to help repair the damage caused to Honduras and Nicaragua by Hurricane Mitch in 1998.

human resources development, technical cooperation and small enterprise development. By the end of 1997 the fund had approved 184 projects to a total of nearly $275 million.

Several of the special trust funds have been set up in response to specific events. A prime example came in December 1998, when the IDB announced a fund to help Honduras and Nicaragua recover from the damage caused by Hurricane Mitch. Current lending priorities include the reduction of poverty, combating corruption, promoting small-scale development, improving the environment, and providing technical assistance to help member countries identify, prepare, and implement new projects.

In 1965 the IDB created the Institute for the Integration of Latin America and the Caribbean, based in Buenos Aires, Argentina, to research all aspects of regional integration and cooperation in international trade and relations with other regions and countries. In 1989 the bank's Inter-American Investment Corporation began operations out of its Washington headquarters, funded by 35 of the IBD member states, with emphasis on investment in small and medium-sized enterprises. The IDB has also established the Inter-American Institute for Social Development (INDES), which since 1995 has trained senior officials in methods to improve social policies and services as part of the attack on poverty and inequality in the region.

ABOVE: The British economist John Maynard Keynes was one of the founding fathers of the International Monetary Fund.

LEFT: At the Bretton Woods conference in 1944 U.S. Treasury Secretary Harry Dexter White put the weight of his country firmly behind the IMF.

The International Monetary Fund (IMF)

Affiliated with the United Nations, the International Monetary Fund's objectives are to promote international trade and to act as a financial safety net for member countries. The IMF was founded in 1946, although it was conceived at the Bretton Woods conference attended by 44 nations in 1944. It was the brainchild of two men—British economist John Maynard Keynes and Harry Dexter White of the U.S. Treasury.

The early 1930s had seen world trade fall by 63 percent as countries devalued their currencies and restricted their imports in an attempt to stabilize their domestic economies. Keynes' and Dexter's idea was to create a permanent international institution that could provide financial assistance to countries with a balance-of-trade problem without them having to resort to devaluations and trade barriers. White wanted the institution to be funded by member countries so that there would be a sense of cooperation and better control of the finances of the country benefiting. Keynes wanted it to be a self-governing world central bank that was able to create its own money and would be free from political influence. In the event the IMF drew on both ideas when it began operations with 35 member countries at its new headquarters in Washington D.C., in 1946. Today the total membership of the IMF is 182.

Raising money for the IMF

The IMF is funded by loans from its member countries' reserves, which can be called on at short notice, effectively counting them as part of its available reserves. When a country joins the IMF, it contributes a sum of money known as a quota subscription. This quota is part of the pool of money that the IMF can draw on and lend to financially troubled members. The quota is also used to calculate how much that country can borrow and its voting power.

The value of the subscription is determined by the IMF itself, based on the country's economic wealth and performance. Richer countries pay more, can borrow more, and have the largest voting rights. The quotas are reviewed every five years and adjusted according to the economic well-being of each country and the needs of the IMF. In 1946 the original 35 members contributed $7.6 billion, and by 1998 the total had risen to $193 billion. Of this the United States contributes the largest amount, about $35 billion, or 18 percent of the total. The U.S. therefore has the largest number of votes.

Who runs the IMF?

The organization of the IMF has two main strata. The Board of Governors, made up usually of either a finance minister or head of a central bank from each member country, formally manages the fund. The board deals mostly with strategy and issues such as the acceptance of new members or the size of the fund. Any increase in quotas has to be approved by 85 percent of the membership.

Reporting to the IMF Governors is the Executive Board, which carries out the policies agreed by the governors and the routine monitoring of the organization. The board comprises 24 directors, with China, France, Germany, Japan, Russia, Saudi Arabia, the United Kingdom, and the United States all represented by permanent directors. The other member states combine their votes, usually in regional groups.

People are often confused about the role of the IMF and its relationship with the World Bank. The important distinction between the two is that the IMF is not a bank but a cooperative arrangement of its members. The members are not dictated to by the IMF itself: it is the members who instruct the IMF to carry out the policies that have been agreed on.

Value judgments

The value of a country's currency is determined when it joins the IMF and is continually monitored thereafter. Up until the 1970s it was pegged to the gold standard, with one ounce of gold fixed at $35. When the gold standard was universally abandoned, the IMF allowed each member to choose a method of determining the exchange rate of its money. This now takes many forms. Some countries allow their currency to float on the world markets, while others peg it to a major currency. For example, a currency can be pegged to the U.S. dollar, and its value will rise and fall with changes in the dollar's value.

How to borrow

If a country gets into severe difficulty with its balance of payments, it can immediately withdraw 25 percent of the quota that it paid in gold or a convertible currency. If this is not enough to enable it to weather the storm, it can apply to the IMF for a loan of up to three times the value of its quota. This is then repayable over a period of three or five years in a currency acceptable to the IMF.

Before any such loan is made, however, the borrowing country must demonstrate how it intends to reform its economy in order to be able to make the repayments. Typically, this will mean the reduction of government expenditure, improvements in monetary policy, and perhaps the privatization of inefficient nationalized industries. Although the IMF will provide technical advice in these circumstances, it is still the member that submits the program of reform for approval, rather than

BELOW: Michel Camdessus, managing director of the IMF, addresses the 1999 annual meeting in Washington, D.C.

the IMF that proposes a plan. Recently the IMF has paid particular attention to the impact of the reforms on the social structure of a country in an effort to ensure that the burden does not fall unfairly on the poorer members of the population.

Recent activities

The 1990s have been the most active decade of the IMF's existence. The early part of that decade saw the breakup of the Soviet Union and the emergence of newly independent republics wishing to change from a centrally planned economy to a market economy. In addition to loaning money, the IMF advised the new governments on such financial structures as setting up central banks and implementing tax systems.

In the mid-1990s a major financial crisis hit Mexico when large capital outflows from the country demonstrated the vulnerability of economies to shifts in the world marketplace. Mexico responded quickly with proposals for reform, and the IMF produced a loan of $17.8 billion to bolster confidence in the country and to avoid the "domino effect" of financial problems that could have affected other member countries.

The Asian crisis came next, with Korea being loaned a record $20.9 billion in 1997, followed by $11.2 billion to Indonesia and more than $4 billion to Thailand. The continuing economic problems in Russia led to that nation receiving a further IMF loan of $11.2 billion in 1998 to supplement an earlier advance of $9.2 billion. The extra burden that this has placed on the IMF's funds has led to an increase in its quotas.

Criticisms of the IMF

Not everyone, however, is happy with the way the IMF, and equally the World Bank, function. The major criticism is that the IMF has crippled many developing nations with debts that they have no realistic chances of paying back in full and that the repayments are sucking essential capital from the countries that need it most. There is thus a growing movement to cancel all Third World debt, not only from pressure groups but also from some governments.

Critics also suggest that despite the IMF's avowed desire to achieve social justice, the poor of the indebted countries will remain poor unless money is channeled into projects that support self-sustainable lifestyles. Large

ABOVE: The inaugural meeting of the IMF on September 11, 1947 in London, England.

projects such as dam building, the critics claim, often do little to improve the quality and quantity of water available to the indigenous population. Dam building is also environmentally destructive, as are many projects involving agricultural export production and forestry.

Many commentators have also expressed concern about the difficulty of gaining access to information about the workings and dealings of the IMF. Consequently there is a growing demand for the IMF to submit to greater public accountability in the decision-making process, particularly for the people of the countries that are receiving the loans.

North American Free Trade Agreement (NAFTA)

Expanding on the bilateral free trade agreement between the United States and Canada that became operational from January 1989, the North American Free Trade Agreement was signed in December 1992 and came into effect on January 1, 1994. The terms of NAFTA stipulate the gradual removal of almost all restrictions on trade and investment between the United States, Canada, and Mexico—countries with a joint population of some 370 million and a combined GNP of more than $6 trillion.

Under NAFTA Mexico would open its financial sector to U.S. and Canadian investment, with all restrictions to be removed by 2007. Existing barriers to investment were removed in most economic sectors, although exemptions were made for petroleum products in Mexico, airlines and radio stations in the United States, and cultural areas in Canada. In 1998 the fifth meeting of the tripartite ministerial Free Trade Commission, held in Paris, France, removed tariffs on more than 600 goods, from chemicals to toys. Some of them were agreed on up to 10 years earlier than originally expected.

The establishment of NAFTA was not, however, a universally popular decision. U.S. labor unions—afraid of losing their jobs if U.S. firms decided to relocate in Mexico to exploit much cheaper costs—demonstrated their resistance throughout the buildup to the signing of the treaty. Mexicans meanwhile worried that NAFTA would lead to their economy being dominated more than ever by powerful U.S. multinational producers and financial services giants.

Indeed, in 1998 opposition sectors in Mexico began complaining of the destructuring of the country's economy. While Mexican

Special Drawing Rights (SDRs)

During the 1960s it appeared that world economic growth would slow down since there were not enough reserves to fund its expansion. This was due to the fact that gold and U.S. dollars were the principal reserves; but gold was in short supply, and it was impossible to count on the United States to spend more dollars abroad indefinitely. The IMF member governments therefore chartered the IMF to create a new asset, known as a special drawing right (SDR), which members could add to the reserves of foreign currency and gold held by their central banks. The value of the SDR was designated as an average of the world's five major currencies. There are now more than 20 billion SDRs, worth more than $30 billion, which account for approximately 2 percent of world reserves.

exports had impressively doubled under NAFTA, reaching $123 billion in 1997 to outstrip the total of the four Mercosur countries (Argentina, Brazil, Paraguay, and Uruguay), more than 80 percent of the value of those exports was controlled by fewer than 300 companies, most of which were multinationals. Little benefit was trickling down to the local level, and imports rose steadily, reaching $121 million that same year.

Meanwhile, in June 1996 both Mexico and Canada announced they were referring the United States Helms-Burton legislation, which provides for punitive measures against foreign companies that trade with Cuba, to the Free Trade Commission on the grounds that it contravenes NAFTA rules.

Widening the scope of NAFTA

In 1993, mainly as a result of lobbying campaigns, the new U.S. government negotiated "side agreements" with its two partners concerning workers' rights and the environment. Under the North American Agreement on Labor Cooperation (NAALC) a Commission for Labor Cooperation was established in Dallas, Texas, to check on the implementation of these labor accords. This body is empowered to impose trade sanctions of up to $20 million, but only in cases of national legislation concerning child labor, the minimum wage, or health or safety standards.

The same year also saw the establishment of two bilateral organizations involving the United States and Mexico. The North

American Development Bank (NADB) finances projects along the border from its headquarters in San Antonio, Texas. By February 1999 the NADB had authorized capital outlays of $3 billion, funded equally by both countries. A Border Environmental Cooperation Commission (BECC) was set up to coordinate projects and monitor the environmental impact of the agreement along the U.S.-Mexican border.

On the wider ecological front, a Commission for Environmental Cooperation (CEC) would try to ensure that economic expansion and development were not damaging to the environment in NAFTA countries. Panels of experts have powers to impose trade sanctions and fines, but only in the United States and Mexico. Opposition to these measures came from Canada, which would enforce NAFTA regulations through its own legal system. Based in Montreal, Canada, the CEC also funds the North American Fund for Environmental Cooperation (NAFEC), established in 1995 to support community environmental projects.

NAFTA expansion

As early as December 1994 the three NAFTA members formally asked Chile to seek membership in their union. Chile already had extensive bilateral agreements with Mexico and began negotiating similar deals with Canada, while the United States was its dominant trading partner. Despite the commencement of formal discussions on Chilean entry in June 1995, however, the U.S. Congress has repeatedly refused to sanction a "fast-track" proposal for such an expansion of NAFTA. Argentina and Colombia have also made repeated approaches to establish agreements with the new common market.

In April 1998 the heads of state from 34 countries met in Santiago, Chile, and agreed to begin negotiations to set up a Free Trade Area of the Americas (FTAA). The plan was that such an organization would exist alongside the previously established subregional trade associations, including NAFTA, rather than supersede them. The negotiating process was scheduled to finish at a meeting in Mexico City on December 31, 2004, under the joint presidency of the United States and Brazil.

NAFTA has few direct parallels with the European Community (EC). The latter evolved gradually from an industrial platform comprising six nations, none of which was economically preeminent, into a wide-ranging economic union of 15 countries, 12 of which now use a single currency. Despite Canada's stability and Mexico's recent progress, the North American free trade area is naturally led by the most powerful economy in the group, that of the United States. Washington calls the shots—Congress every bit as much as the NAFTA headquarters—and will continue to do so for the foreseeable future.

ABOVE: The signing of the original NAFTA agreement in San Antonio, Texas on October 7, 1992. Among those pictured are U.S. President George Bush, Carlos Salinas de Gortari, President of Mexico, and Brian Mulroney, Prime Minister of Canada.

Organization for Economic Cooperation and Development (OECD)

Originating in 1961, the OECD is an inter-governmental organization the main aims of which are to improve and sustain the economic health of its 29 member countries. The OECD evolved from an earlier organization, the Organization for European Economic Cooperation (OEEC), which was founded after World War II to implement the Marshall Plan. (The Marshall Plan was a scheme by which the United States provided aid to Europe to facilitate economic recovery.)

By 1961 the OEEC had largely achieved its aims, and both the status and the title of the organization were changed. When the United States and Canada joined, the word "European" was dropped and "Development" added. It was the United States' wish that the now prosperous European countries should join it in providing economic support to developing countries. Japan (1964), Finland (1969), Australia (1971), and New Zealand (1973) joined the founder countries, bringing the total membership to 24.

What does the OECD do?

The OECD is funded by member countries and has no financial resources of its own. It does not give grants nor make loans, but is essentially a data-gathering and advisory body that provides a forum for policymakers to compare their points of view and experience and to act as a catalyst in problem solving.

Research is carried out by the organization into a wide range of subjects, including economic policy, development strategy, international trade, agriculture, energy, environmental issues, science, technology, and education. Several independent or semi-independent agencies are associated with it, including the Nuclear Energy Agency, the International Energy Agency, the Center for International Research and Innovation, and the European Conference of Ministers of Transport.

Who runs the OECD?

The governing body of the OECD is its council, which is responsible for general policy. It is composed of a representative of each member country and meets once a year at ministerial level, but twice a month at the "official" level, which is attended by permanent representatives. Most of the OECD's work is

BELOW: Not everyone in the United States loves NAFTA. In a speech in Washington, D.C,. in 1993 U.S. electrical union workers president William Bywater warned of possible job losses as a result of the agreement.

The NAFTA agreement

ABOVE: Under the terms of NAFTA the ownership of Mexican oilfields–which are presently a state monopoly—will be open to offers from other member countries from 2004.

A comprehensive plan for the elimination of trade barriers between the United States, Canada, and Mexico—known as the North American Free Trade Agreement (NAFTA) was signed in 1992 and came into effect on January 1, 1994. Its major provisions are as follows:

● Tariffs on 10,000 customs goods to be eliminated over a 15-year period; 50 percent of U.S. exports to Mexico to be duty-free within five years.

● Tariffs on all farm products to be eliminated over 15 years; domestic agricultural price-support systems may continue if they do not distort trade.

● Tariffs on automobiles to be phased out over 10 years; for a vehicle to qualify as duty-free, at least 62.5 percent of its value must have been produced in North America. This provision to come into effect by 2002.

● Most tariffs on textiles to be phased out over five years; "rule of origin" provision requires most garments to be made from fabric and yarn produced in North America.

● Trucks to have free access on crossborder routes and throughout the three member countries by 1999.

● All three countries to ease the restrictions on movement of business executives and professionals; barriers for limiting Mexican migration into the United States remain in force.

● U.S. and Canadian banks may acquire Mexican commercial banks, accounting for up to 8 percent of the industry's capital; all limits on ownership to end in 2004.

● While Mexico continues to bar foreign ownership of its oil fields, from 2004 U.S. and Canadian firms may bid on contracts offered by Mexican oil (and electricity) monopolies.

● The agreement cannot be used to overrule national or state laws on the environment, health, or safety.

● Special judges have jurisdiction to resolve disagreements between members within strict timetables.

Statistical note on U.S. trade surpluses and deficits

Between 1992 and 1997 the United States' deficit on its trade balance with Canada increased from $8 billion to nearly $16.5 billion. Over the same period the United States' balance of trade with Mexico moved from a surplus of $5.381 billion to a deficit of $14.549 billion.

prepared and carried out by some 200 working parties or committees that draw on the OECD's vast database resources.

The OECD and Eastern Europe

After the political and economic upheavals that took place in Eastern Europe and the former Soviet republics in the 1980s, the OECD set up the Center for Cooperation with Economies in Transition (CCET) in 1990 with the aim of helping former communist states progress to market economies. A year later a program was inaugurated to consider the particular needs of the Czech Republic, Hungary, Poland, and Slovakia. Some of these countries, and others, have now become full members of the OECD—the Czech Republic (1995), Hungary and Poland (1996). Mexico and South Korea have also joined, in 1995 and 1996 respectively.

Organization of Petroleum Exporting Countries (OPEC)

Created to protect the interests of its members, OPEC is a protectionist cartel (*see* page 63, The world economy) established in 1960 as a forum for 13 of the world's largest oil-exporting nations to discuss the levels at which each member should set its production quotas in order to control export prices. OPEC also coordinates and determines the level of aid granted by members to developing countries. There were originally 13 members of OPEC—Algeria, Ecuador, Gabon, Indonesia, Iran, Iraq, Kuwait, Libya, Nigeria, Qatar, Saudi Arabia, the United Arab Emirates, and Venezuela—but there are now only 12 since the resignation of Ecuador. At the height of OPEC's power in the 1970s these countries together accounted for 60 percent of total world crude oil production and 90 percent of total world exports. After the 1970s oil crisis, however, the use of alternative sources of oil and the drilling of wells in non-OPEC nations such as Norway and the United Kingdom caused OPEC's share of world market to fall to 40 percent by the end of the 20th century.

The World Bank

The World Bank is the everyday name given to the International Bank for Reconstruction and Development (IBRD). The World Bank was originally set up with the IMF after the United Nations Monetary Conference at Bretton Woods, New Hampshire, in 1944. The aim of the IBRD was to support the physical and economic reconstruction of Europe after the devastation of World War II. The Marshall Plan, however, supplied most of the necessary early support for Europe's recovery, and the emphasis in the IBRD's role shifted toward the provision of assistance for developing countries. Today only developing countries are able to borrow from the World Bank.

Who owns the World Bank?

The IBRD has 180 member countries, all of which are also members of the IMF. Each member country subscribes to the IBRD's capital stock according to an allocated quota that is based on its individual economic strength. The main capital shareholders are the United States, Japan, the United Kingdom, Germany, and France. Capital contributions are increased at regular intervals, and at the end

BELOW: World leaders at the OECD summit in Venice, Italy in 1980. Those pictured (left to right) are Japanese Foreign Minister Saburo Okita, Canadian Prime Minister Pierre Trudeau, West German Chancellor Helmut Schmidt, French President Valery Giscard D'Estaing, Italian Prime Minister Francesco Cossiga, U.S. President Jimmy Carter, British Prime Minister Margaret Thatcher, and EC Commission President Roy Jenkins.

The Marshall Plan

On June 5, 1947, George C. Marshall, the U.S. secretary of state, made a famous speech at Harvard University in which he pledged material support for the war-ravaged countries of Europe, provided that their governments drew up programs "designed to place Europe on its feet economically." Although strictly known as the European Recovery Program, the initiative that resulted from this speech is now known universally as the Marshall Plan.

OECD auspices

The Organization for European Economic Cooperation (OEEC)—the forerunner of the OECD (*see* page 107)—was charged with creating the conditions that would ensure a fair and equitable division of U.S. funds and free up trade within and to and from Europe. Although there is no doubt that the implementation of the Marshall Plan greatly increased U.S. influence in Europe, that was not its principal aim. The United States' intention was always primarily altruistic—to help stabilize the traditionally hostile countries of Europe to such an extent that war was no longer a viable instrument of their foreign policy.

Soviet suspicion

The Soviet Union and other Eastern European countries were invited to join the new organization, but the Soviet distrust of Western economic values ensured that it, and its satellite Communist nations—Bulgaria, Czechoslovakia, East Germany, Hungary, Poland, and Romania—decided not to join.
There were originally 17 recipients of Marshall Plan aid through the OEEC, with Spain the last nation to take advantage of the funds in 1959.

ABOVE: U.K. politicians welcome the first shipment of sugar from the Caribbean to England under the Marshall Plan for U.S. postwar aid to Europe.

of the financial year 1998 the total subscribed capital amounted to about $200 billion. Less than 5 percent of this total is actually paid into the IBRD, but the bank can call on its members for payment if necessary. So far this has never happened.

Who runs the World Bank?
The IBRD is governed by the Board of Governors, who meet once a year. Each member country appoints a governor and an alternate governor. They are usually the country's finance minister, the governor of the central bank, or someone who has a say in the country's fiscal policy. At the annual meetings they decide on policy issues and changes in the level of capital stock, admit or suspend member countries, endorse statements and budgets, and agree on the distribution of the IBRD's net income.

Day-to-day running of the World Bank is undertaken by the 24-member Board of Executive Directors. Each of the five biggest stakeholders—the United States, Japan, the United Kingdom, Germany, and France—appoints an executive director. The remaining 19 board members are elected by constituency. Some countries, such as China and Russia, have formed single-country constituencies, while some smaller countries, which have geographic and economic links with each other, have joined together to form multicountry constituencies. The executive board of the IBRD meets to oversee such bank business as approving loans and guarantees, administrative costs, establishing country assistance strategies, and endorsing all borrowing and finance decisions. IBRD loans are made to national governments or must be guaranteed by the government concerned, and are financed by bond issues on the world capital markets. The first was issued in 1947 for $13.5 million. Total IBRD lending to 1998 was more than $400 billion.

The World Bank Group includes four other agencies—The International Development Association (IDA), the International Finance Corporation (IFC), the Multilateral Investment Guarantee Agency (MIGA), and the International Center for Settlement of Investment Disputes (ICSID).

The International Center for Settlement of Investment Disputes (ICSID)

The ICSID was founded in 1966 to promote the growth of private foreign investment for economic development by creating facilities

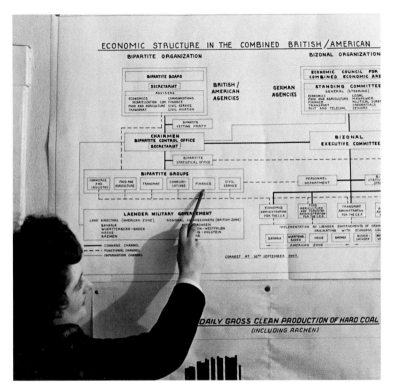

for settling disputes between governments and foreign investors from different contracting states. By June 30, 1998, 129 nations had ratified the ICSID convention to become members, and another 15 had signed it. Disputes may occur in a range of areas, including banking, industry, agriculture, construction, mining, energy, health, and tourism.

The governing body of the center is an administrative council that includes one representative from each contracting state. All members have equal voting rights under the nonvoting chair of the president of the World Bank. ICSID is based at the World Bank headquarters in Washington, D.C., where it also carries out research, advising, and publishing in foreign investment law.

International Development Association (IDA)

The IDA is administered by the World Bank and is open to all its members. Inaugurated in 1960, it makes loans to the poorest member countries, those whose balance of payments could not bear the burden of the repayments required for World Bank lending. The limit for 1997 was an annual per capita GNP figure of less than $925 at 1995 rates. The terms are more favorable than those of the World Bank, interest-free and with credit periods of 35 or 40 years, plus another 10-year "period of grace."

In the year ending June 30, 1998—during which some 80 nations were eligible for IDA assistance—the agency's credits totaled more

ABOVE: After World War II, Germany was partitioned, and the economic reconstruction of the western part of the country carefully monitored by the United States and the United Kingdom.

than $7.5 billion. Most of this money went to assist the poorest countries, with 37.5 percent of the total going to Africa and 33.9 percent to South Asia. The largest single recipient nation was India, followed by Ethiopia and Bangladesh. Priority is given to education, reduction of poverty, elimination of child labor, AIDS treatment and awareness programs, and environmental protection.

IDA funds are made up largely of members' subscriptions and are replenished periodically by the wealthier nations of the World Bank. In 1998, during the IDA's 12th replenishment round, 39 donor countries undertook to provide $11.6 billion. taking the total funds available for lending over the period July 1999 to June 2002 to around $20.5 billion.

The International Finance Corporation (IFC)

The IFC was founded in 1956 as a member of the World Bank Group to encourage and stimulate economic growth in the developing nations by mobilizing capital in international finance markets, financing private sector investment, and providing technical advice and assistance to governments and commercial concerns. It finances new ventures and helps existing ones expand or diversify. In order to qualify, projects must benefit the economy of the country involved, comply with IFC environmental guidelines—and be profitable for investors.

Funds are provided by a variety of mediums, including long-term loans, guarantees, equity investments, and standby financing. In the year ending June 30, 1998, approved IFC project financing amounted to $5.9 billion for over 300 projects. The IFC usually limits its financing to between 5 percent and 15 percent of the cost of a project, but it may take up to a 35 percent holding in specific ventures. Around 80 percent of its income is borrowed from the international market through private placements or public bond issues, with the remaining 20 percent supplied by the World Bank.

As of January 1999 the IFC had 174 member states. Its headquarters in Washington, D.C., runs seven regional departments and 10 specialized departments. There are 21 regional and resident missions worldwide, plus

BELOW: A Muslim farmer in Heshijia boils water using a primitive solar heating device. This village in China's southwestern Qinghai Province was subsequently relocated to more productive land in Dulan County, a move funded by the World Bank.

special representatives and advisers in the United Kingdom, France, Germany, Norway, Japan, and Australia.

Multinational Investment Guarantee Agency (MIGA)

MIGA is the insurance arm of the World Bank. Established in 1988 with authorized capital of over $1 billion, its mandate is to encourage the flow of direct foreign investment to and among developing member countries through the mitigation of risk in the form of investment insurance.

While it gives advice to governments on creating the climate for foreign investment, its main role is to guarantee investments (up to 90 percent) against noncommercial risks such as armed conflict, civil unrest, and expropriation by the host government. Before guaranteeing any investment, MIGA ensures that it is commercially viable, aids the development process, and does not harm the environment. During the year ending June 30, 1998, MIGA issued 55 contracts (down from 70 the previous year),

with a total value of $831 million. The total investment of these contracts, which created over 8,000 jobs in 26 countries, was $6.1 billion.

By 1999 MIGA had a membership of 149 states, with another 16 countries in the process of fulfilling requirements for membership. Like ICSID and IDA, its offices are located at the World Bank's headquarters in Washington, D.C.

Environmental aid

The World Bank devotes significant funds to the protection of the environment. In 1999 it provided a $10.15 million grant to help preserve the vulnerable ecosystem within the West Tien Shan mountain range in the former Soviet republics of Kazakhstan, Kyrgyzstan, and Uzbekistan. The region contains a wide variety of habitats, from subtropical to tundra, and houses unique and threatened species like the snow leopard, white-clawed bears, and Central Asian goats and wild sheep. The region is also home to hundreds of wild species of medicinal, agricultural, and horticultural plants that represent an important genetic bank for the future.

BELOW: The President of the World Bank, James D. Wolfensohn, at his desk in Manhattan, New York.

Where the money goes

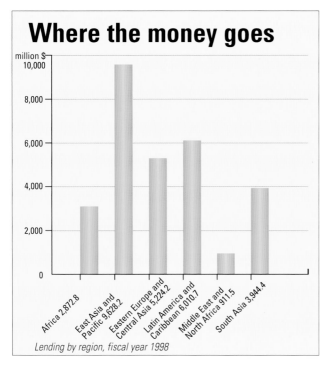

million $

Lending by region, fiscal year 1998

(values: Africa 2,872.8; East Asia and Pacific 9,628.2; Eastern Europe and Central Asia 5,224.2; Latin America and Caribbean 6,010.7; Middle East and North Africa 911.5; South Asia 3,944.4)

How the money is spent

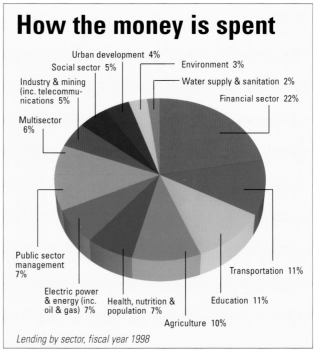

Urban development 4%
Social sector 5%
Industry & mining (inc. telecommunications 5%
Multisector 6%
Public sector management 7%
Electric power & energy (inc. oil & gas) 7%
Health, nutrition & population 7%
Agriculture 10%
Education 11%
Transportation 11%
Financial sector 22%
Water supply & sanitation 2%
Environment 3%

Lending by sector, fiscal year 1998

The World Trade Organization (WTO)

The WTO is the legal and institutional foundation of the modern world's trading system (*see* International trade and finance, page 36). The act that brought it into existence on January 1, 1995, was signed by the trade ministers of 123 countries. By the start of the 21st century WTO membership had grown to 135 nations.

WTO succeeded the General Agreement on Tariffs and Trade (GATT), which had sought since 1948 to reduce worldwide tariffs by negotiation. The 23 original members of GATT were charged with drafting a charter for an International Trade Organization, but it was never ratified and a burgeoning GATT remained the only regime for the regulation of world trade, evolving its own rules and procedures. There were eight "rounds" of GATT negotiations, the last of which began in Montevideo, Uruguay, in 1986.

This "Uruguay Round" lasted almost eight years and was superseded by the start of WTO. When the changeover took place, GATT had 111 contracting members, while another 22 countries applied its rules on a de facto basis. The 500 staff of the GATT secretariat in Geneva now services the WTO, which has no resources of its own outside its modest operating budget (115 million Swiss francs for 1998).

Aims, functions, and organization

The principal aims of the WTO are to liberalize world trade and to put it on a secure footing through an agreed set of trade rules and

ABOVE: Farmers in the developing world have been among the main beneficiaries of investment by international economic organizations.

market access agreements. It thus provides for the progressive reduction of tariffs, duties, quotas, and subsidies on a range of goods and products. By the time the measures of the Uruguay Round are fully implemented—it is intended by 2002—the average duties on manufactured goods will have been reduced from 40 percent to just 3 percent. The WTO also administers a further 29 multilateral agreements in areas such as agriculture, textiles and clothing, dumping, trade in services, and intellectual property. Decisions on all matters are in theory at least ultimately reached by consensus, and there are no procedures for the enforcement of its rules.

Another key part of the agency's role is the surveillance of national trade policies through the Trade Policy Review Mechanism (TPRM). The main objective of the TPRM is to increase understanding of, and reduce complications between, all members' trade policies. The four members with the the largest share of world trade (the European Union, the United States, Japan, and Canada) are reviewed every two years; the next 16 largest member nations are reviewed every four years, and the others every six years, with longer intervals possible for the least developed countries.

The ultimate policymaking body of the WTO is the Ministerial Conference, which is held every two years. The General Council, made up of representatives of all 135 members, reports to the conference; it has 30 subordinate councils and committees, and conducts much of the daily work of the WTO. A Dispute Settlement Body of the council deals with disagreements between members.

The WTO is mandated to cooperate with other international organizations—notably the World Bank and the IMF—in order to pursue greater coherence in making decisions on the global economy. The preparatory committee of the WTO chose not to incorporate the new body into the UN but to develop cooperation agreements with the World Bank and the IMF and to broaden links with the United Nations Conference on Trade and Development (UNCTAD) in research, trade, and technology. The International Trade Center, founded by GATT in 1964, and already operated jointly with UNCTAD since 1968, continues to work on a wide range of Third World development fields, and in 1984 it became an executing agency of the UN Development Program.

Shambles in Seattle

The WTO's third and last ministerial conference of the 20th century, held in Seattle, Washington, revealed severe structural weaknesses and deep divisions in the organization. Most press attention was focused on the disruption caused by 60,000 street demonstrators—a diverse but highly effective alliance of workers, human rights activists, farmers, consumer rights campaigners, aid lobbyists, environmentalists, and anarchists who had coordinated their activities largely via the Internet. But there were also massive problems inside the Convention Center, with the disrupted conference breaking up in disarray and recrimination between members.

Poor organization and lack of preparation did not help matters. Little progress had been made beforehand on the sprawling draft

BELOW: The trade in agricultural produce has long been one of the most important links between Europe and North America. Here cotton from the United States lies in a dock shed at Le Havre, France.

TRIPS to nowhere

A growing source of tension in international economic relations is the widely varying standards in the protection and enforcement of intellectual property rights. They have become increasingly important with the phenomenal but uncontrolled success of the Internet. Linked to this is a lack of rules dealing with trade in counterfeit goods, notably in the clothing, music, and toy industries.

The WTO Agreement on Trade-Related Aspects of Intellectual Property (TRIP) tries to ensure that adequate standards exist in all countries and aims to expand them in a range of areas. They include protection of computer programs (as literary works), tighter protection of integrated circuit designs, definition of trademarks, protection for trade secrets and "know-how" with commercial value, 10-year protection for industrial designs, and 20-year patents for all inventions.

ABOVE: Like all owners of intellectual property, the popular musician and songwriter Sting needs legal protection to prevent his work being pirated.

legislation (only two paragraphs had been finalized), and the failure to agree on an advance agenda proved a crucial mistake.

Negotiations were handicapped by a number of compounding factors, including the perceived self-interest of the hosts. U.S. Trade Secretary Charlene Barshefsky was accused of arrogance by delegates from the developing countries, and President Bill Clinton of trying to hijack the event for his own purposes: instead of providing political impetus to the world's poorest nations with a package granting them duty-free access to lucrative U.S. markets, Clinton was accused of playing to his domestic audience by noting the need for labor standards to be part of WTO deals. Another problem was the blatant maneuverings of the big trading blocs—notably the EU, the United States, and the Cairns group of agricultural free traders—to stitch up mutually beneficial deals, often behind closed doors, and thus excluding Third World nations.

Lessons must be learned from Seattle if the WTO is not to slide further into disorder and disrepute. Already widely acknowledged as overbearing, secretive, bureaucratic (its rules run to 36,000 pages in English), and above all totally unaccountable to any supervisory body, it is increasingly perceived as a closed shop run by an alliance of powerful national governments and rich transnational companies. Critics say the agency has to realize that global trade means global participation: the WTO must become more democratic, inclusive, and accountable. To benefit a greater number of people, the process should be weighted more toward informed pressure groups and away from vested political and corporate interests.

Nevertheless, Seattle may prove a mere blip on the graph of WTO's relentless growth and progress. As *Time* magazine put it on the eve of the conference: "The WTO is both traffic cop and top court of the global economy. With China's bid for admission, the organization seems set to extend its gospel of no-pain, no-gain capitalism across the planet."

The debate over globalization

Ironically, perhaps, in the home of Boeing and Microsoft, two of the biggest American exporters, the real target of the Seattle demonstrators was not the reduction of trade barriers in itself but the globalization process it represents. Somewhat unfairly, the WTO was by now acting as a magnet for resistance to globalization, attracting the blame for all the ills it is thought to cause.

Critics regard globalization as no more than the latest form of colonialism in which corporate profits are put before the quality of life of the people who produce the goods that make those profits; governments, in the developing world as well as in the West, are held equally responsible for aiding and abetting the growth of the transnationals.

Supporters of globalization claim that the process, with assistance from the liberalization of trade afforded by GATT and WTO, has brought cheaper imports, new technologies, the incentive of greater competition, and above all, faster growth; greater prosperity is the key to improving working conditions and the environment—in all countries. Indeed, most free traders assert that far too many barriers still exist, and that self-seeking protectionism is always threatening to return to kill the golden goose of globalization.

SEE ALSO:

• Volume 5, page 25: The developing world

• Volume 5, page 35: Exchange rates

• Volume 5, page 41: Free trade and protectionism

• Volume 5, page 78: Oligopoly and oligopolistic competition

• Volume 5, page 110: Trade and international trade

• Volume 5, page 112: Transitional economies

• Volume 6, page 86: The West in the 20th century

• Volume 6, page 106: Today and tomorrow

Glossary

accounts records of earnings, expenditure, assets, and liabilities kept by individuals, firms, and governments.

balance of payments a record of a country's international trade, borrowing, and lending.

balance of trade an indicator of a country's financial condition produced by subtracting the value of imports from the value of exports.

balance sheet a list of assets and liabilities that shows the financial condition of a firm, individual, or other economic unit.

barter a system of trading in which goods are exchanged for other goods rather than for money

black market an illegal part of the economy that is not subject to regulation or taxation and that often deals in high-priced, illegal or scarce commodities.

bond a legal obligation to pay a specified amount of money on a specified future date.

boom and bust a phrase that describes a period of wild swings in economic activity between growth and contraction.

business cycle the periodic but irregular fluctuation in economic activity, usually measured by GDP, which rises and falls for reasons economists do not fully understand.

capital the physical assets owned by a household, firm, or government, such as equipment, real estate, and machinery. Capital is also used to mean financial capital, or money used to finance a business venture.

capitalism an economic system based on private ownership and enterprise and the free market. Capitalism has been the dominant economic system in the western world since around the 16th century.

central bank a public organization, sometimes subject to government influence but often independent, established to oversee and regulate a country's monetary and financial institutions.

commodity a primary product such as coffee, cotton, copper, or rubber. In economics, "commodity" is also used to describe a good or service created by the process of production.

communism a political doctrine based on the ideas of the philosopher Karl Marx that seeks to establish social equality through central regulation of the economic activity and communal ownership. *See also* planned economies.

comparative advantage the advantage gained by a producer—an individual, firm, or government—if they can produce a good at a lower opportunity cost than any other producer.

consumer good an economic good or commodity that is bought for use by a household rather than by industry, for example.

consumer price index (CPI) an economic indicator based on the price of a range of goods and services to calculate an average for expenditure of a U.S. family.

cost benefit analysis the appraisal of a project or policy, for example, by comparing all the social and financial costs with the social and financial benefits arising from that project or policy.

curve a line plotted between points on a graph; an economic curve can be a straight line.

deflation a general downward movement of prices.

demand the desire for a particular good or service backed by the ability to pay for it.

depression a deep trough in the business cycle, usually marked by high prices and high unemployment.

developing country a poor country that is undergoing a process of economic modernization, typically including an increase of GDP through the development of an industrial and commercial base.

economies of scale factors which cause the average cost of producing a good to fall as output increases.

entrepreneurship the ability to perceive opportunities in the market and assemble factors of production to exploit those opportunities.

externality a cost or benefit falling on a third party as the result of an economic activity which is not accounted for by those carrying out that activity.

factors of production the productive resources of an economy, usually defined as land, labor, entrepreneurship, and capital.

fiscal policy the attempts a government makes to maintain economic balance by altering its spending on goods or services or its revenue-raising through taxation.

foreign exchange rate the rate at which one country's money is exchanged for another. The rate is often used as a measure of the relative strengths and weaknesses of different economies.

free trade international trade that is not subject to barriers such as tariffs or quotas.

gross domestic product (GDP) the total value of the final output within the borders of a particular economy.

gross national product (GNP) GDP plus the income accruing to domestic residents from investments abroad, less the income earned in the domestic market by foreigners abroad.

inflation an upward movement in the general level of prices.

interest the amount earned by savers or investors on their deposit or investment or paid by borrowers on their loan. The amount of interest is determined by the interest rate.

Keynesianism an economic doctrine based on the theories of J. M. Keynes that advocates government intervention through fiscal policy to stabilize fluctuations in the economy.

labor the workforce who provide muscle or brainpower for economic activity.

laissez-faire a French term for "let it do," originally used in classic economics to describe an economy with no government intervention.

land land and all natural resources such as oil, timber, and fish.

liquidity a measure of how easily an asset can be converted into cash.

macroeconomics the name given to the study of the economy as a whole rather than with the detailed choices of individuals or firms. *See also* microeconomics.

the market an arrangement which facilitates the buying and selling of a good, service, or factor of production. In a free market the prices which result from this are regulated by the laws of supply and demand rather than by external constraints.

mercantilism an economic policy popular in Europe from the 16th to the 18th centuries that stressed the importance of exports to earn reserves of gold and silver and used high tariffs to prevent imports.

microeconomics the study of individual households and firms, the choices they make in individual markets, and the effects of taxes and government regulation. *See also* macroeconomics.

monetarism an economic doctrine that regards the quantity of money in an economy as the main determinant of aggregate demand. As such, attempts by government to increase output by stimulating demand will only result in inflation.

monetary policy the attempt to regulate inflation and economic activity by varying the money supply and interest rates. Monetary policy is often the responsibility of a central bank.

money supply the amount of liquid assets in an economy that can easily be exchanged for goods and services, usually including notes, coins, and bank deposits that can be transferred by writing checks.

monopoly a market in which there is only one supplier of a good or service for which there is no close substitute.

neocolonialism a relationship between a country and a former colony in which the business interests of the first continue to dominate the economy of the latter.

opportunity cost the best alternative that must be given up when an economic choice is made.

planned economy an economy in which production and distribution are determined by a central authority, such as a ruler or a government.

private sector that part of an economy in which activity is decided and the means of production owned by individuals or firms rather than government. *See also* public sector.

productivity the ratio between the input of resources such as capital and labor and the resulting output of goods and services.

protectionism an economic doctrine that attempts to protect domestic producers by placing tariffs on imported goods.

public sector that part of an economy owned by a government or other public bodies such as state administrations.

recession a severe contraction of economic activity marked by two successive quarters of falling GDP.

specialization the decision by an individual, firm, or government to produce only one or a few goods or services.

sustainable development a form of economic growth that seeks to use renewable rather than finite resources and to minimize the permanent damage done to the environment by economic activity.

supply the quantity of a good or service available for sale at a particular price.

taxes and tariffs compulsory charges placed on economic activity by governments. Taxes might be placed on wealth or income, on business profits, as a sales tax on transactions, or as license fees on activities such as driving. Tariffs are taxes placed on imports into a country.

trusts anticompetitive alliances formed among businesses to force prices up and bring costs down. Trusts were outlawed in the United States by the Sherman Antitrust Act of 1890.

unemployment the condition of adult workers who do not have jobs and are looking for employment.

wealth the total assets of a household, firm, or country less its total liabilities.

welfare state a system of welfare provision by a government to keep its citizens healthy and free from poverty. Welfare provisions typically include free health care, insurance against sickness or unemployment, old age pensions, disability benefits, subsidized housing, and free education.

The World's Economies, 1996

	Population (millions)	GDP $m		Population (millions)	GDP $m		Population (millions)	GDP $m
Afghanistan	20.9	12.8	Germany	81.9	2,364.6	Nigeria	115.0	27.6
Albania	3.4	2.7	Ghana	17.8	6.2	North Korea	22.5	21.5
Algeria	28.8	43.7	Greece	10.5	120.0	Norway	4.3	151.2
Angola	11.2	3.0	Guadeloupe	0.4	3.7	Oman	2.3	15.3
Argentina	35.2	295.1	Guatemala	10.9	16.0	Pakistan	140.0	63.6
Armenia	3.6	2.4	Guinea	7.5	3.8	Panama	2.7	8.2
Australia	18.1	367.8	Guinea-Bissau	1.1	0.3	Papua New Guinea	4.5	5.0
Austria	8.1	226.5	Haiti	7.3	2.3	Paraguay	5.0	9.2
Azerbaijan	7.6	3.6	Honduras	5.8	4.0	Peru	23.9	58.7
Bahamas	0.3	3.5	Hong Kong	6.2	153.3	Philippines	69.3	83.3
Bahrain	0.6	5.7	Hungary	10.0	44.3	Poland	38.6	124.7
Bangladesh	120.1	31.2	Iceland	0.3	7.2	Portugal	9.8	100.9
Barbados	0.3	2.0	India	944.6	357.8	Puerto Rico	3.7	30.3
Belarus	10.3	22.5	Indonesia	200.5	213.4	Qatar	0.6	7.5
Belgium	10.2	268.6	Iran	70.0	132.9	Réunion	0.7	2.9
Benin	5.6	2.0	Iraq	20.6	21.9	Romania	22.7	36.2
Bermuda	0.1	2.1	Ireland	3.6	62.0	Russia	148.1	356.0
Bhutan	1.8	0.3	Israel	5.7	90.3	Rwanda	5.4	1.3
Bolivia	7.6	6.3	Italy	57.2	1,140.5	Saudi Arabia	18.8	125.3
Bosnia	3.6	3.3	Jamaica	2.5	4.1	Senegal	8.5	4.9
Botswana	1.5	4.8	Japan	125.4	5,149.2	Serbia, Montenegro	10.3	15.7
Brazil	161.1	709.6	Jordan	5.6	7.1	Sierra Leone	4.3	0.9
Brunei	0.3	4.6	Kazakhstan	16.8	22.2	Singapore	3.4	93.0
Bulgaria	8.5	9.9	Kenya	27.8	8.7	Slovakia	5.3	18.2
Burkina Faso	10.8	2.4	Kirgizstan	4.5	2.5	Slovenia	1.9	18.4
Burundi	3.2	1.1	Kuwait	1.7	31.0	Somalia	9.8	3.6
Cambodia	10.3	3.1	Laos	5.0	1.9	South Africa	42.4	132.5
Cameroon	13.6	8.4	Latvia	2.5	5.7	South Korea	45.3	483.1
Canada	29.7	569.9	Lebanon	3.1	12.1	Spain	39.7	563.2
Central African			Lesotho	2.1	1.3	Sri Lanka	18.1	13.5
Republic	3.3	1.0	Liberia	2.2	2.3	Sudan	27.3	10.7
Chad	6.5	1.0	Libya	5.6	23.1	Suriname	0.4	1.3
Chile	14.4	70.1	Lithuania	3.7	8.5	Swaziland	0.9	1.1
China	1,232.1	906.1	Luxembourg	0.4	18.9	Sweden	8.8	227.3
Colombia	36.4	80.2	Macau	0.4	7.4	Switzerland	7.2	313.7
Congo	46.8	5.7	Macedonia FYR	2.2	2.0	Syria	14.6	16.8
Congo-Brazzaville	2.7	1.8	Madagascar	15.4	3.4	Taiwan	21.5	275.0
Costa Rica	3.5	9.1	Malawi	9.8	1.8	Tajikistan	5.9	2.0
Cote d'Ivoire	14.0	9.4	Malaysia	20.6	89.8	Tanzania	30.8	5.2
Croatia	4.5	18.1	Mali	11.1	2.4	Thailand	58.7	177.5
Cuba	11.0	18.0	Malta	0.4	3.3	Togo	4.2	1.3
Cyprus	0.8	8.9	Martinique	0.4	3.9	Trinidad and Tobago	1.3	5.0
Czech Republic	10.3	48.9	Mauritania	2.3	1.1	Tunisia	9.2	17.6
Denmark	5.2	168.9	Mauritius	1.1	4.2	Turkey	61.8	177.5
Dominican Republic	8.0	12.8	Mexico	92.7	341.7	Turkmenistan	4.2	4.3
Ecuador	11.7	17.5	Moldova	4.4	2.5	Uganda	20.3	5.8
Egypt	63.3	64.3	Mongolia	2.5	0.9	Ukraine	51.6	60.9
El Salvador	5.8	9.9	Morocco	27.0	34.9	United Arab Emirates	2.3	44.6
Eritrea	3.3	0.8	Mozambique	17.8	1.5	United Kingdom	58.1	1,152.1
Estonia	1.5	4.5	Myanmar	45.9	63.4	United States	269.4	7,433.5
Ethiopia	58.2	6.0	Namibia	1.6	3.6	Uruguay	3.2	18.5
Fiji	0.8	2.0	Nepal	22.0	4.7	Uzbekistan	23.2	23.5
Finland	5.1	119.1	Netherlands	15.6	402.6	Venezuela	22.3	67.3
France	58.3	1,533.6	Netherlands Antilles	0.2	1.9	Vietnam	75.2	21.9
Gabon	1.1	4.4	New Zealand	3.6	57.1	West Bank & Gaza	0.8	3.9
Gambia, The	1.1	0.4	Nicaragua	4.2	1.7	Yemen	15.7	6.0
Georgia	5.4	4.6	Niger	9.5	1.9	Zambia	8.3	3.4
						Zimbabwe	11.4	6.8

Further reading

Allen, L. *Encyclopedia of Money*. Santa Barbara, CA: ABC-Clio, 1999.

Ammer C., and Ammer, D. S. *Dictionary of Business and Economics*. New York: MacMillan Publishing Company, 1986.

Atrill, P. *Accounting and Finance for Non-Specialists*. Engelwood Cliffs, NJ: Prentice Hall, 1997.

Baker, J.C. *International Finance: Management, Markets, and Institutions*. Engelwood Cliffs, NJ: Prentice Hall, 1997.

Baites, B. *Europe and the Third World: From Colonisation to Decolonisation, 1500-1998*. New York: St. Martins Press, 1999.

Bannock, G., Davis, E., and Baxter, R.E. *The Economist Books Dictionary of Economics*. London: Profile Books, 1998.

Barilleaux, R.J. *American Government in Action: Principles, Process, Politics*. Englewood Cliffs, NJ: Prentice Hall, 1995.

Barr, N. *The Economics of the Welfare State*. Stanford, CA: Stanford University Press, 1999.

Barro, R.J. *Macroeconomics*. New York: John Wiley & Sons Inc, 1993.

Baumol, W.J., and Blinder, A.S. *Economics: Principles and Policy*. Forth Worth, TX: Dryden Press, 1998.

Begg, D., Fischer, S., and Dornbusch, R. *Economics*. London: McGraw-Hill, 1997.

Black, J.A. *Dictionary of Economics*. New York: Oxford University Press, 1997.

Blau, F.D., Ferber, M.A., and Winkler, A.E. *The Economics of Women, Men, and Work*. Engelwood Cliffs, NJ: Prentice Hall PTR, 1997.

Boyes, W. and Melvin, M. *Fundamentals of Economics*. Boston, MA: Houghton Mifflin Company, 1999.

Bradley, R.L., Jr. *Oil, Gas, and Government: The U.S. Experience*. Lanham, MD: Rowman and Littlefield, 1996.

Brewer, T.L., and Boyd, G. (ed.). *Globalizing America: the USA in World Integration*. Northampton, MA: Edward Elgar Publishing, 2000.

Brownlee, W.E. *Federal Taxation in America: A Short History*. New York: Cambridge University Press, 1996.

Buchholz, T.G. *From Here to Economy: A Short Cut to Economic Literacy*. New York: Plume, 1996.

Burkett, L., and Temple, T. *Money Matters for Teens Workbook: Age 15-18*. Moody Press, 1998.

Cameron, E. *Early Modern Europe: an Oxford History*. Oxford: Oxford University Press, 1999.

Chown, J.F. *A History of Money: from AD 800*. New York: Routledge, 1996.

Coleman, D.A. *Ecopolitics: Building a Green Society* by Daniel A. Coleman Piscataway, NJ: Rutgers University Press, 1994.

Cornes, R. *The Theory of Externalities, Public Goods, and Club Goods*. New York: Cambridge University Press, 1996.

Dalton, J. *How the Stock Market Works*. New York: Prentice Hall Press, 1993.

Daly, H.E. *Beyond Growth: the Economics of Sustainable Development*. Boston, MA: Beacon Press, 1997.

Dent, H.S., Jr. *The Roaring 2000s: Building the Wealth and Lifestyle you Desire in the Greatest Boom in History*. New York: Simon and Schuster, 1998.

Dicken, P. *Global Shift: Transforming the World Economy*. New York: The Guilford Press, 1998.

Economic Report of the President Transmitted to the Congress. Washington, D.C.: Government Publications Office, 1999.

Elliott, J. H. *The Old World and the New, 1492-1650*. Cambridge: Cambridge University Press, 1992.

Epping, R.C. *A Beginner's Guide to the World Economy*. New York: Vintage Books, 1995.

Ferrell, O.C., and Hirt, G. *Business: A Changing World*. Boston: McGraw Hill College Division, 1999.

Frankel, J.A. *Financial Markets and Monetary Policy*. Cambridge, MA: MIT Press, 1995.

Friedman, D.D. *Hidden Order: The Economics of Everyday Life*. New York: HarperCollins, 1997.

Friedman, M., and Friedman, R. *Free to Choose*. New York: Penguin, 1980.

Glink, I.R. *100 Questions You Should Ask About Your Personal Finances*. New York: Times Books, 1999.

Green, E. *Banking: an Illustrated History*. Oxford: Diane Publishing Co., 1999.

Greer, D.F. *Business, Government, and Society*. Engelwood Cliffs, NJ: Prentice Hall, 1993.

Griffin, R.W., and Ebert, R.J. *Business*. Engelwood Cliffs, NJ: Prentice Hall, 1998.

Hawken, P., et al. *Natural Capitalism: Creating the Next Industrial Revolution*. Boston, MA: Little Brown and Co., 1999.

Hegar, K.W., Pride, W.M., Hughes, R.J., and Kapoor, J. *Business*. Boston: Houghton Mifflin College, 1999.

Heilbroner, R. *The Worldly Philosophers*. New York: Penguin Books, 1991.

Heilbroner, R., and Thurow, L.C. *Economics Explained: Everything You Need to Know About How the Economy Works and Where It's Going*. Touchstone Books, 1998.

Hill, S.D. (ed.). *Consumer Sourcebook*. Detroit, MI: The Gale Group, 1999.

Hirsch, C., Summers, L., and Woods, S.D. *Taxation : Paying for Government*. Austin, TX: Steck-Vaughn Company, 1993.

Houthakker, H.S. *The Economics of Financial Markets*. New York: Oxford University Press, 1996.

Kaufman, H. *Interest Rates, the Markets, and the New Financial World*. New York: Times Books, 1986.

Keynes, J.M. *The General Theory of Employment, Interest, and Money*. New York: Harcourt, Brace, 1936.

Killingsworth, M.R. *Labor Supply*. New York: Cambridge University Press, 1983.

Kosters, M.H. (ed.). *The Effects of Minimum Wage on Employment*. Washington, D.C.: AEI Press, 1996.

Krugman, P.R., and Obstfeld, M. *International Economics: Theory and Policy*. Reading, MA: Addison-Wesley Publishing, 2000.

Landsburg, S.E. *The Armchair Economist: Economics and Everyday Life*. New York: Free Press (Simon and Schuster), 1995.

Lipsey, R.G., Ragan, C.T.S., and Courant, P.N. *Economics*. Reading, MA: Addison Wesley, 1997.

Levine, N. (ed.). *The U.S. and the EU: Economic Relations in a World of Transition*. Lanham, MD: University Press of America, 1996.

MacGregor Burns, J. (ed.). *Government by the People*. Engelwood Cliffs, NJ: Prentice Hall, 1997.

Magnusson, L. *Mercantilism*. New York: Routledge, 1995.

Mayer, T., Duesenberry, J.S., and Aliber, R.Z. *Money, Banking and the Economy*. New York: W.W. Norton and Company, 1996.

Mescon, M.H., Courtland, L.B., and Thill, J.V. *Business Today*. Engelwood Cliffs, NJ: Prentice Hall, 1998.

Morris, K.M, and Siegel, A.M. *The Wall Street Journal Guide to Understanding Personal Finance*. New York: Lightbulb Press Inc, 1997

Naylor, W. Patrick. *10 Steps to Financial Success: a Beginner's Guide to Saving and Investing*. New York: John Wiley & Sons, 1997.

Nelson, B.F., and Stubb, C.G. (ed.) *The European Union : Readings on the Theory and Practice of European Integration*. Boulder, CO: Lynne Rienner Publishers, 1998.

Nicholson, W. *Microeconomic Theory: Basic Principles and Extensions*. Forth Worth, TX: Dryden Press, 1998.

Nordlinger, E.A. *Isolationism Reconfigured: American Foreign Policy for a New Century*. Princeton, NJ: Princeton University Press, 1996.

Painter, D.S. *The Cold War*. New York: Routledge, 1999.

Parkin, M. *Economics*. Reading, MA: Addison-Wesley, 1990.

Parrillo, D.F. *The NASDAQ Handbook*. New York: Probus Publishing, 1992.

Porter, M.E. *On Competition*. Cambridge, MA: Harvard Business School Press, 1998.

Pounds, N.J.G. *An Economic History of Medieval Europe*. Reading, MA: Addison-Wesley, 1994.

Pugh, P., and Garrett, C. *Keynes for Beginners*. Cambridege, U.K.: Icon Books, 1993.

Rima, I.H. *Labor Markets in a Global Economy: An Introduction*. Armonk, NY: M.E. Sharpe, 1996.

Rius *Introducing Marx*. Cambridge, U.K.: Icon Books, 1999.

Rosenberg. J.M. *Dictionary of International Trade*. New York: John Wiley & Sons, 1993.

Rye, D.E. *1,001 Ways to Save, Grow, and Invest Your Money*. Franklin Lakes, NJ: Career Press Inc, 1999.

Rymes, T.K. *The Rise and Fall of Monetarism: The Re-emergence of a Keynesian Monetary Theory and Policy*. Northampton, MA: Edward Elgar Publishing, 1999.

Sachs, J.A., and Larrain, F.B. *Macroeconomics in the Global Economy*. Englewood Cliffs, NJ: Prentice Hall, 1993.

Shapiro, C., and Varian, H.R. *Information Rules: A Strategic Guide to the Network Economy*. Cambridge, MA: Harvard Business School, 1998.

Smith, A. *An Inquiry into the Nature and Causes of the Wealth of Nations*, Edwin Cannan (ed.). Chicago: University of Chicago Press, 1976.

Spulber, N. *The American Economy: the Struggle for Supremacy in the 21st Century*. New York: Cambridge University Press, 1995.

Stubbs, R., and Underhill, G. *Political Economy and the Changing Global Order*. New York: St. Martins Press, 1994.

Teece, D.J. *Economic Performance and the Theory of the Firm*. Northampton, MA: Edward Elgar Publishing, 1998.

Thurow, L.C. *The Future of Capitalism: How Today's Economic Forces Shape Tomorrow's World*. New York: Penguin, USA, 1997.

Tracy, J.A. *Accounting for Dummies*. Foster City, CA: IDG Books Worldwide, 1997.

Tufte, E. R. *Political Control of the Economy*. Princeton, NJ: Princeton University Press, 1978.

Varian, H.R. *Microeconomic Analysis*. New York: W. W. Norton and Company, 1992.

Veblen, T. *The Theory of the Leisure Class (Great Minds Series)*. Amherst, NY: Prometheus Books, 1998.

Wallis, J., and Dollery, B. *Market Failure, Government Failure, Leadership and Public Policy*. New York: St. Martin's Press, 1999.

Weaver, C.L. *The Crisis in Social Security: Economic and Political Origins*. Durham, NC: Duke University Press, 1992.

Werner, W., and Smith, S.T. *Wall Street*. New York: Columbia University Press, 1991.

Weygandt, J.J., and Kieso, D.E. (ed.). *Accounting Principles*. New York: John Wiley & Sons Inc, 1996.

Williams, J. (ed.). *Money. A History*. London: British Museum Press, 1997.

Websites

Consumer Product Safety Commission: http://www.cpsc.gov/

Equal Employment Opportunity Commission: http://www.eeoc.gov/

Environmental Protection Agency: http://www.epa.gov/

Federal Reserve System: http://www.federalreserve.gov/

Federal Trade Commission: http://www.ftc.gov/

Food and Drug Administration: http://www.fda.gov/

The Inland Revenue Service: http://www.irs.gov/

Occupational Health and Safety Administration: http://www.osha.gov/

Social Security Administration: http://www.ssa.gov/

The U.S. Chamber of Commerce: http://www.uschamber.com

The U.S. Labor Department: http://www.dol.gov/

The U.S. Treasury Department: http://www.treas.gov/

Picture Credits

Index

Page numbers in **bold** refer to main articles; those in *italics* refer to pictures or their captions.

Fluvanna County High School
1918 Thomas Jefferson Parkway
Palmyra, VA 22963